Harmony

By Leen Margot

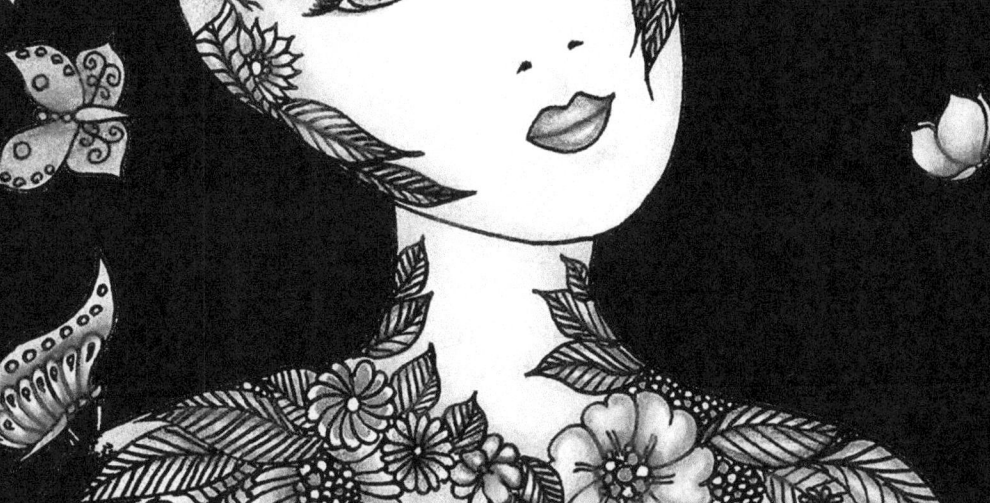

Presented by
Global Doodle Gems

Coloring by
Laety Esperanza

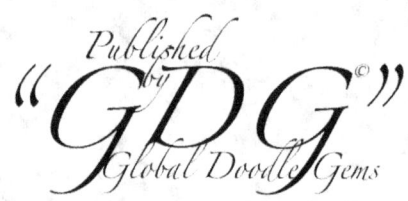

Share your colored versions with us ! We love seeing your results and hearing from you we are social !

The Official FB book page, stay on top of what we have in the works !
www.facebook.com/globaldoodlegems

The Community group, share your colored pages, meet the artists, enjoy exclusive freebies, take part in community Charity books and so much more......
www.facebook.com/groups/globaldoodlegems/

Follow us on Twitter.... @GlobalDoodlegem

We are on Instagram too
@globaldoodlegems for instagram

...and if you are not social like that we have a blog
globaldoodlegems.wordpress.com

Copyright © 2015 Global Doodle Gems

All rights are reserved by Global Doodle Gems.

Duplication of pages for personal use are allowed. You are invited to color the pages then scan/post your coloured versions to social networks, mentioning the book title and author/artist (Global Doodle Gems).

All artwork and images are protected by copyright laws. This book or any portion thereof may not, otherwise, be reproduced and/or distributed or transmitted without the express written permission of the artist/publisher of Global Doodle Gems.

All of us from the Global Doodle Gems wish you a colortastic time and look forward to seeing your wonderful color results online !

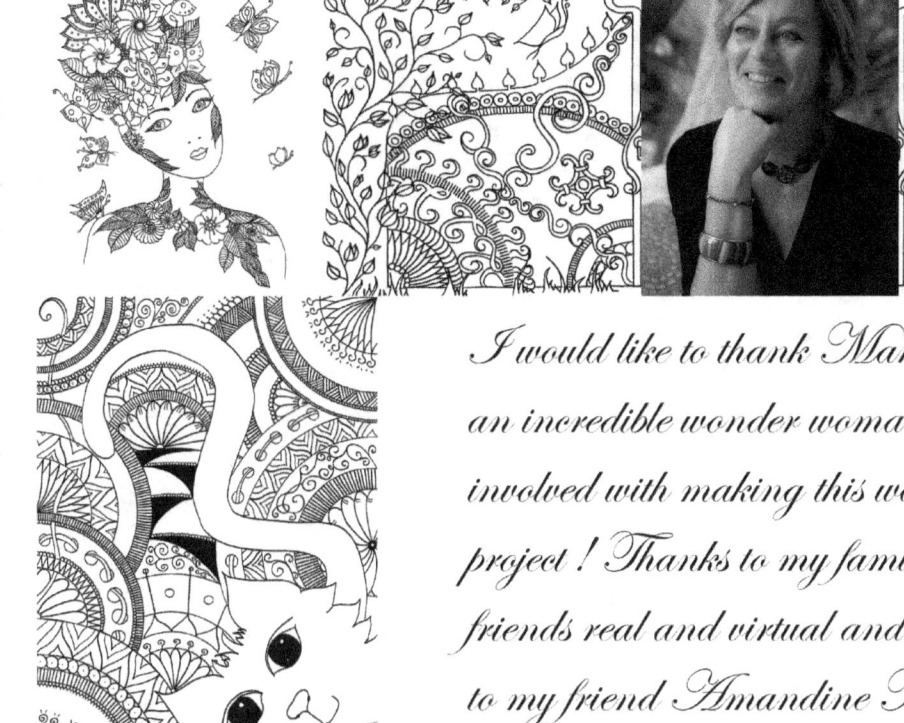

Harmony

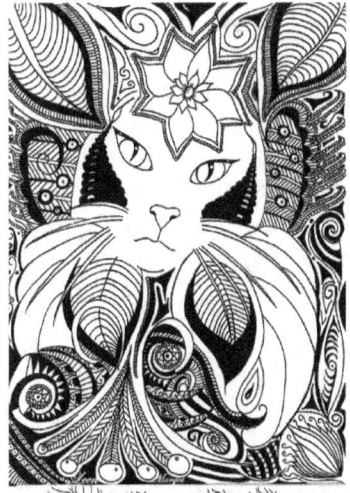

Harmonie

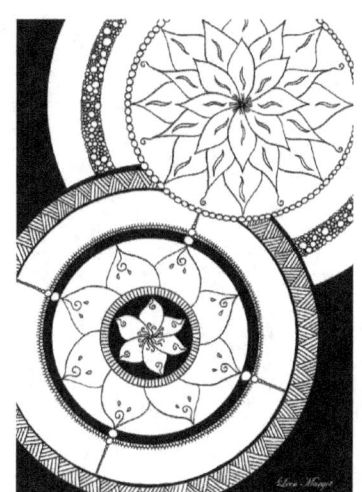

I would like to thank Maria Wedel, an incredible wonder woman who was involved with making this wonderful project! Thanks to my family and my friends real and virtual and especially to my friend Amandine Mimin. A special thanks to two passionate colorists: Laety Esperanza for the cover and Vero Pignot for the back cover.

I hope you will have many quiet and peaceful moments when coloring my designs! I'm sure you will do wonderful coloring ;-)

Leen

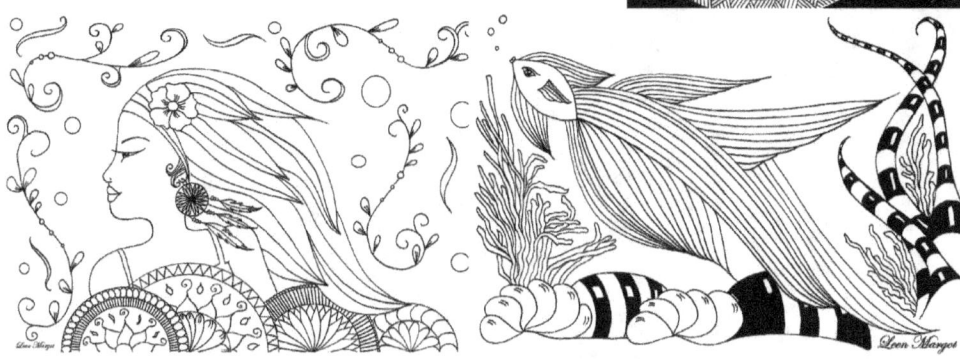

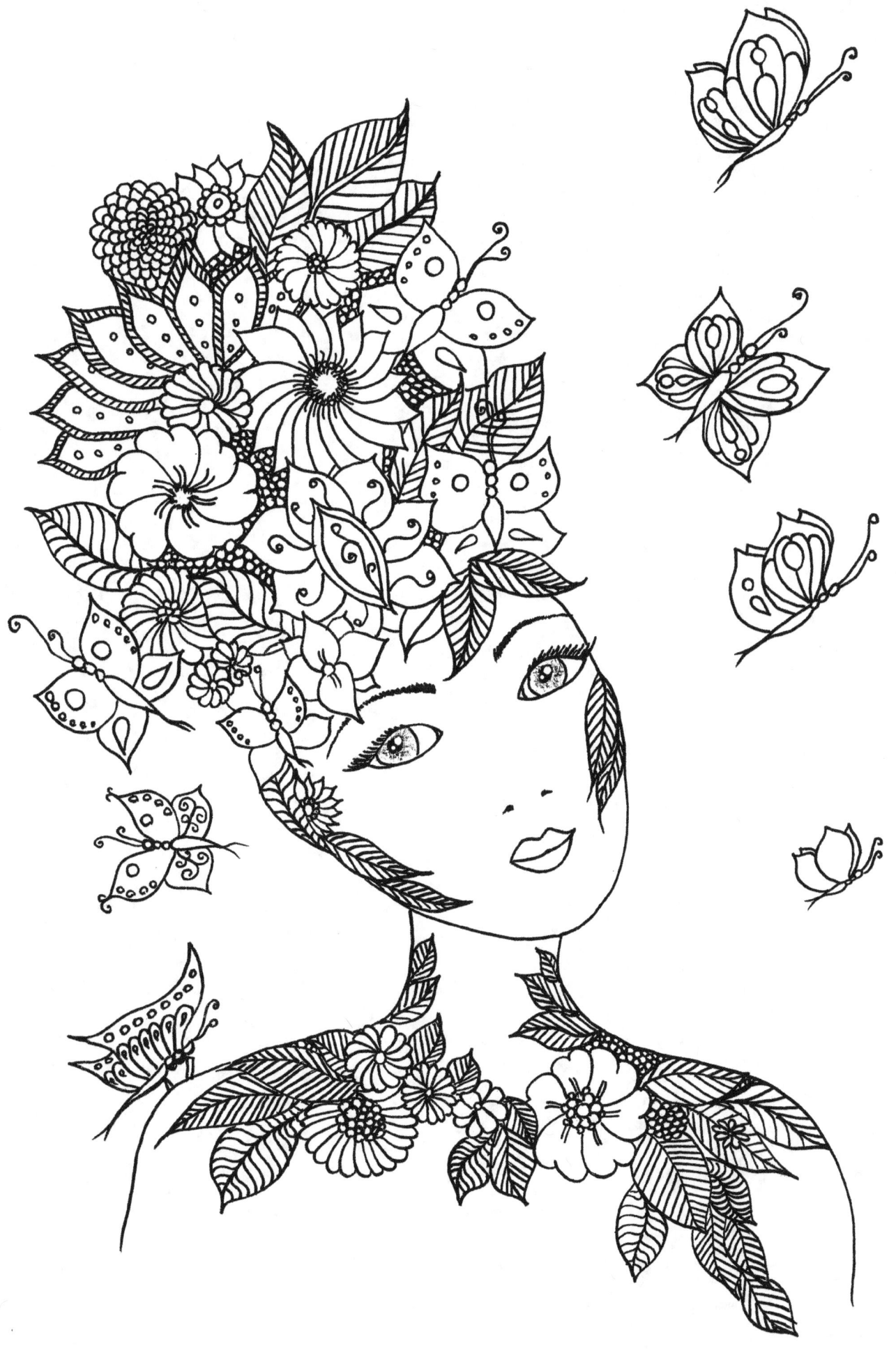

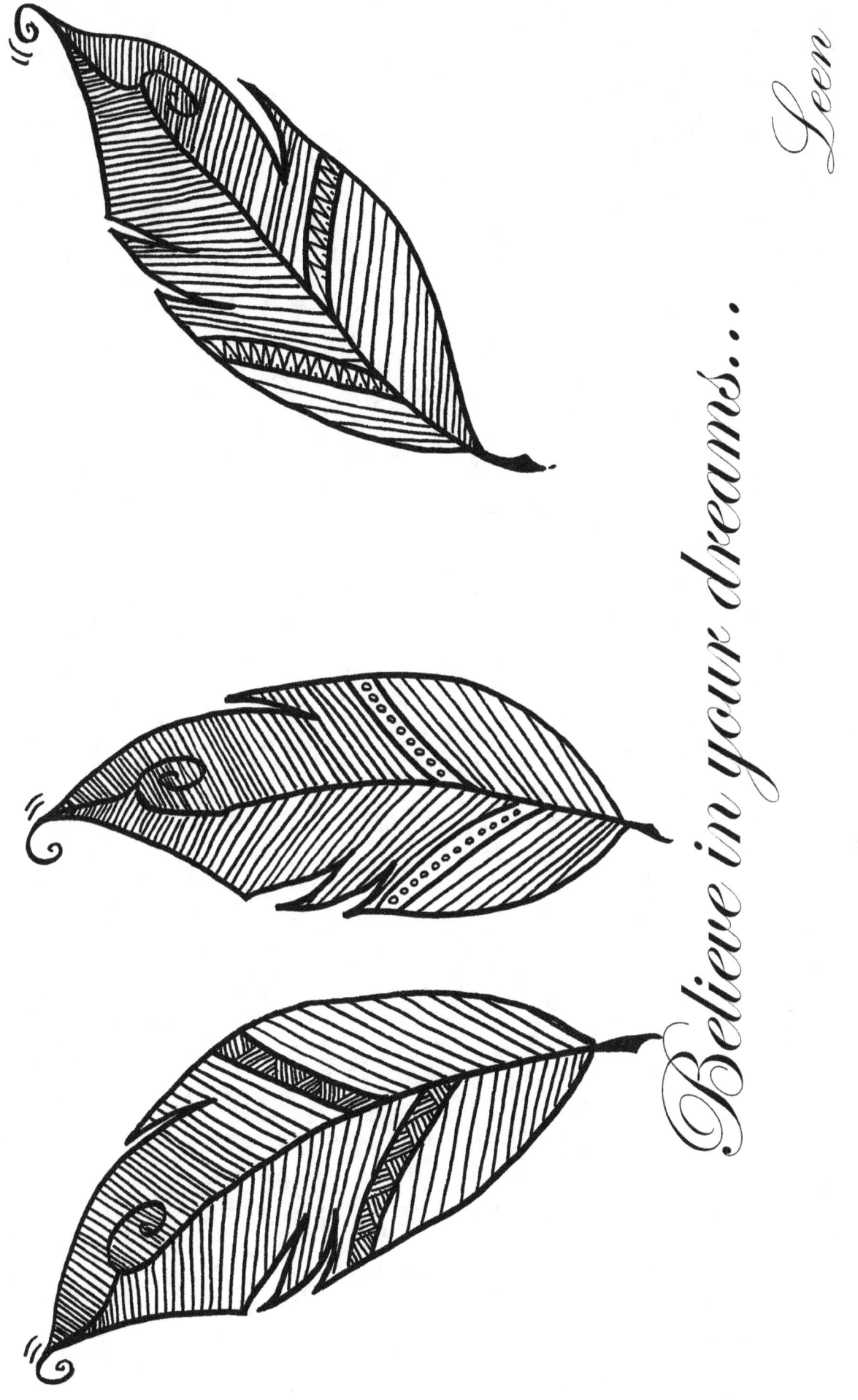

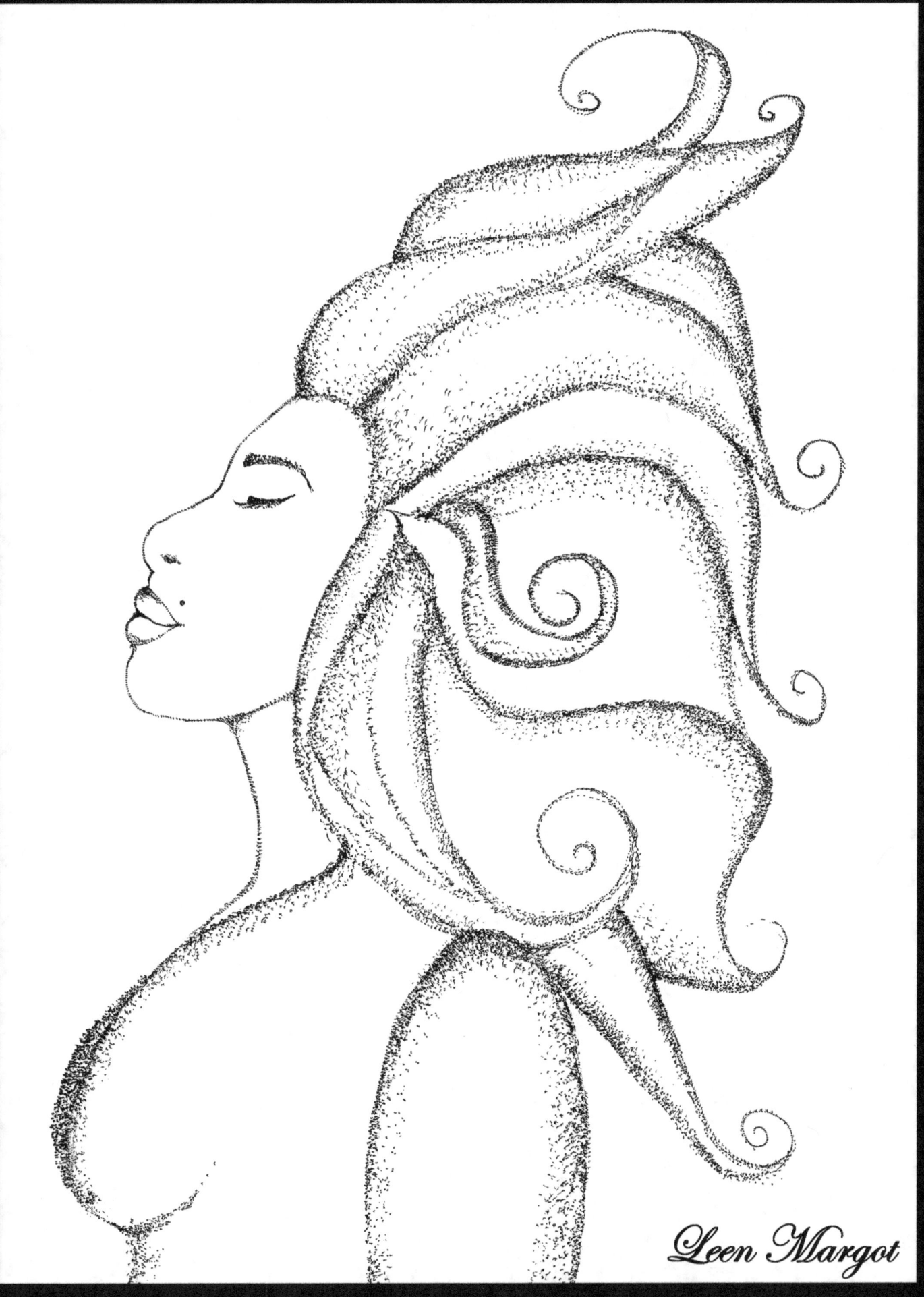

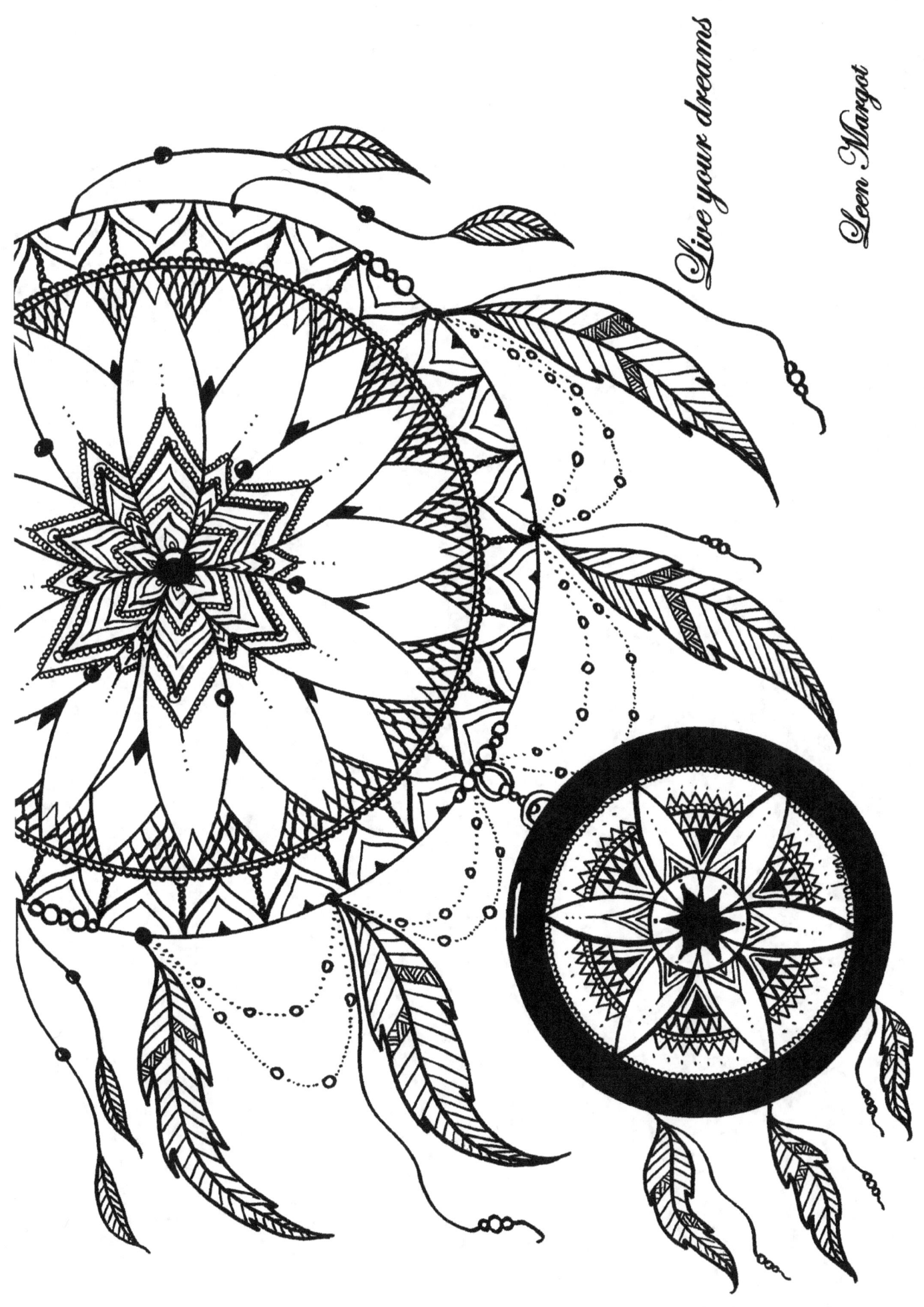

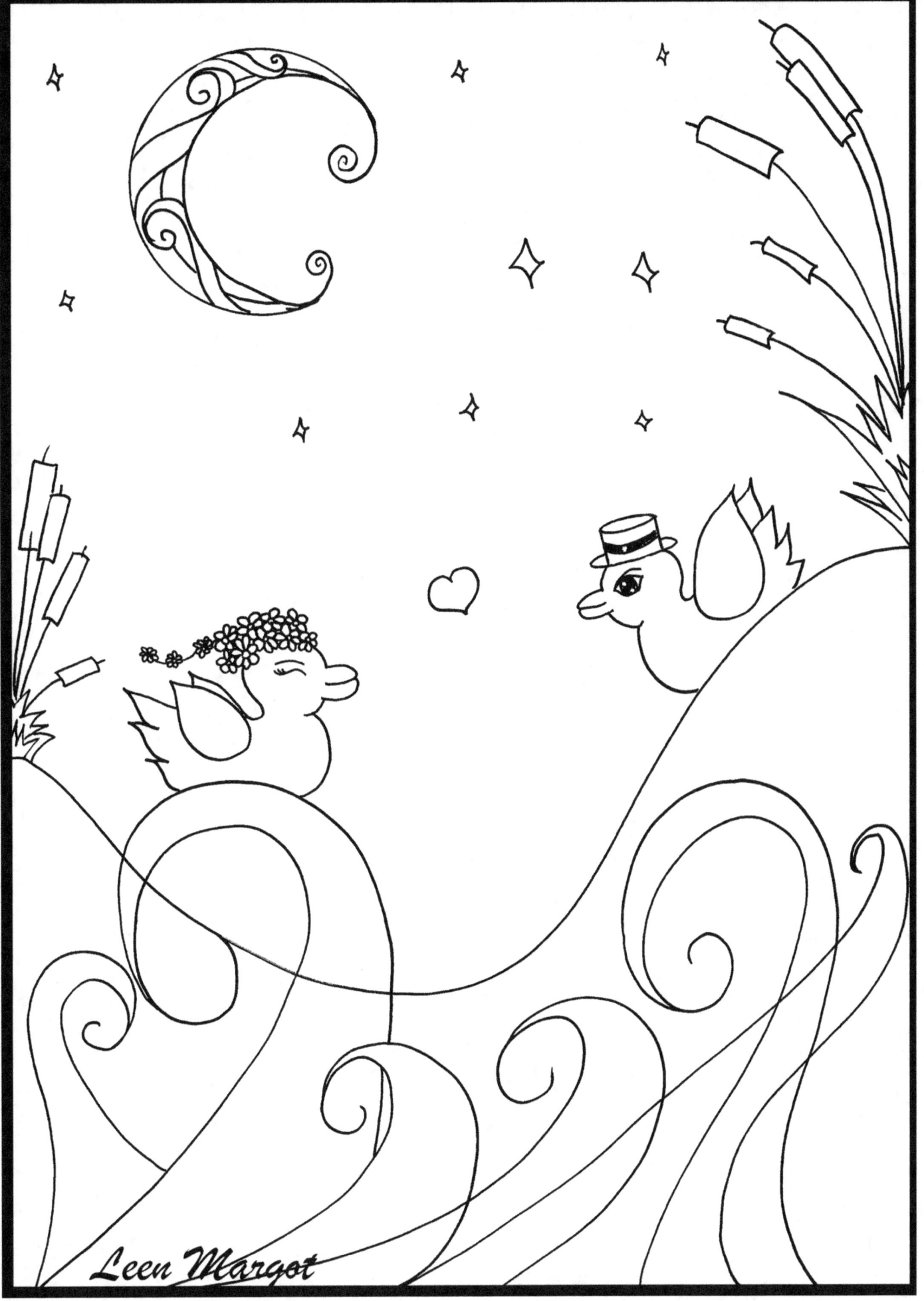

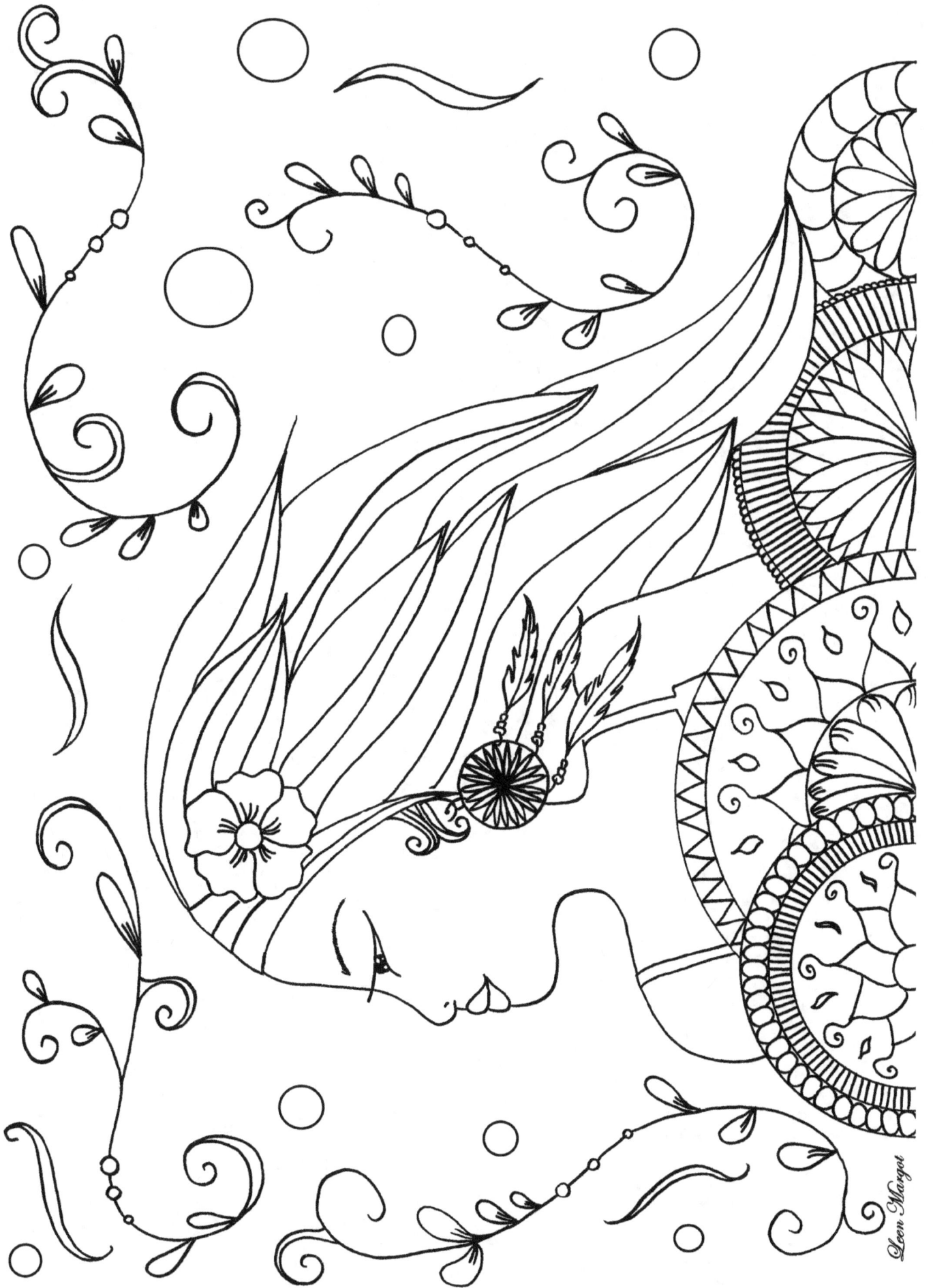

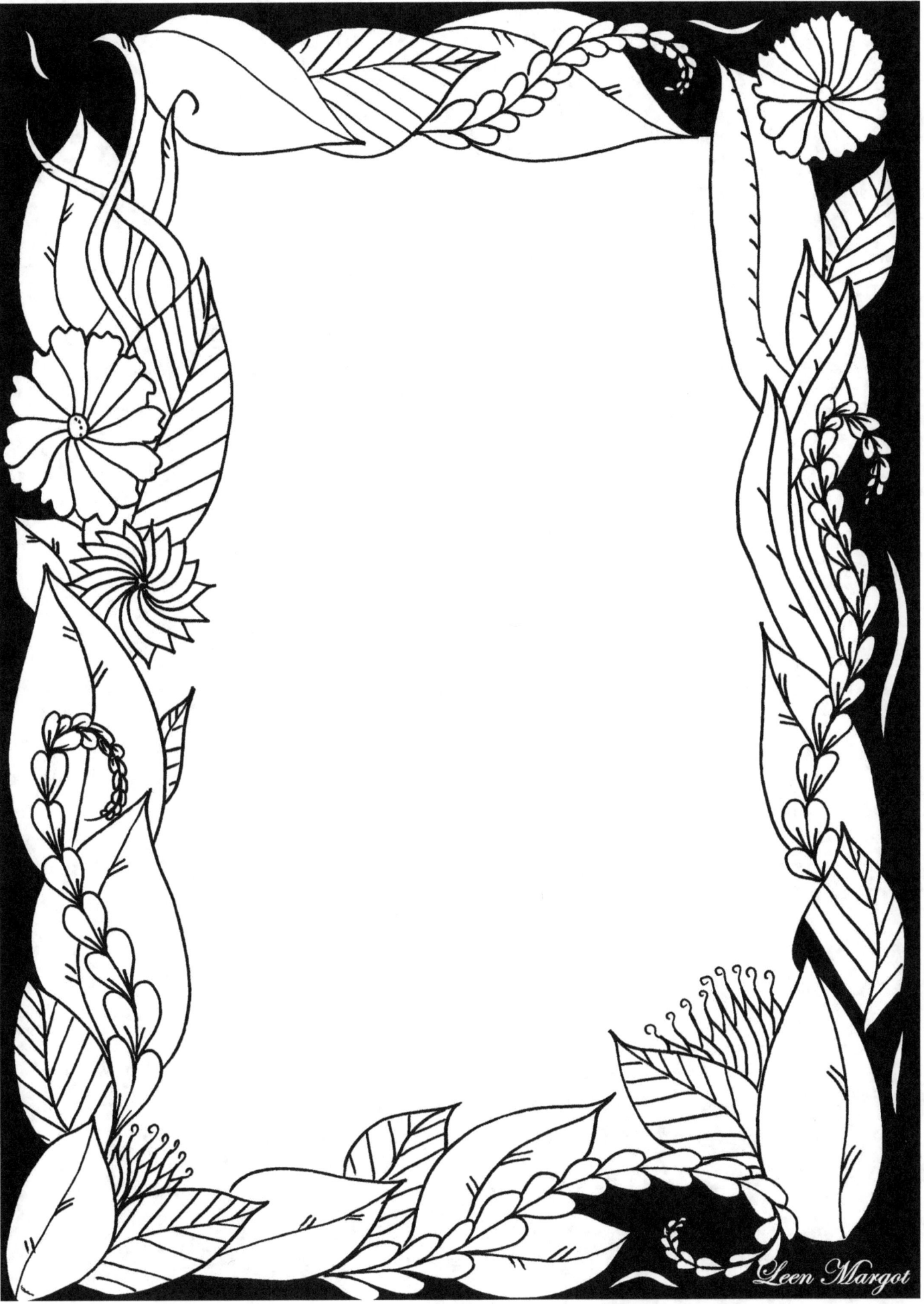

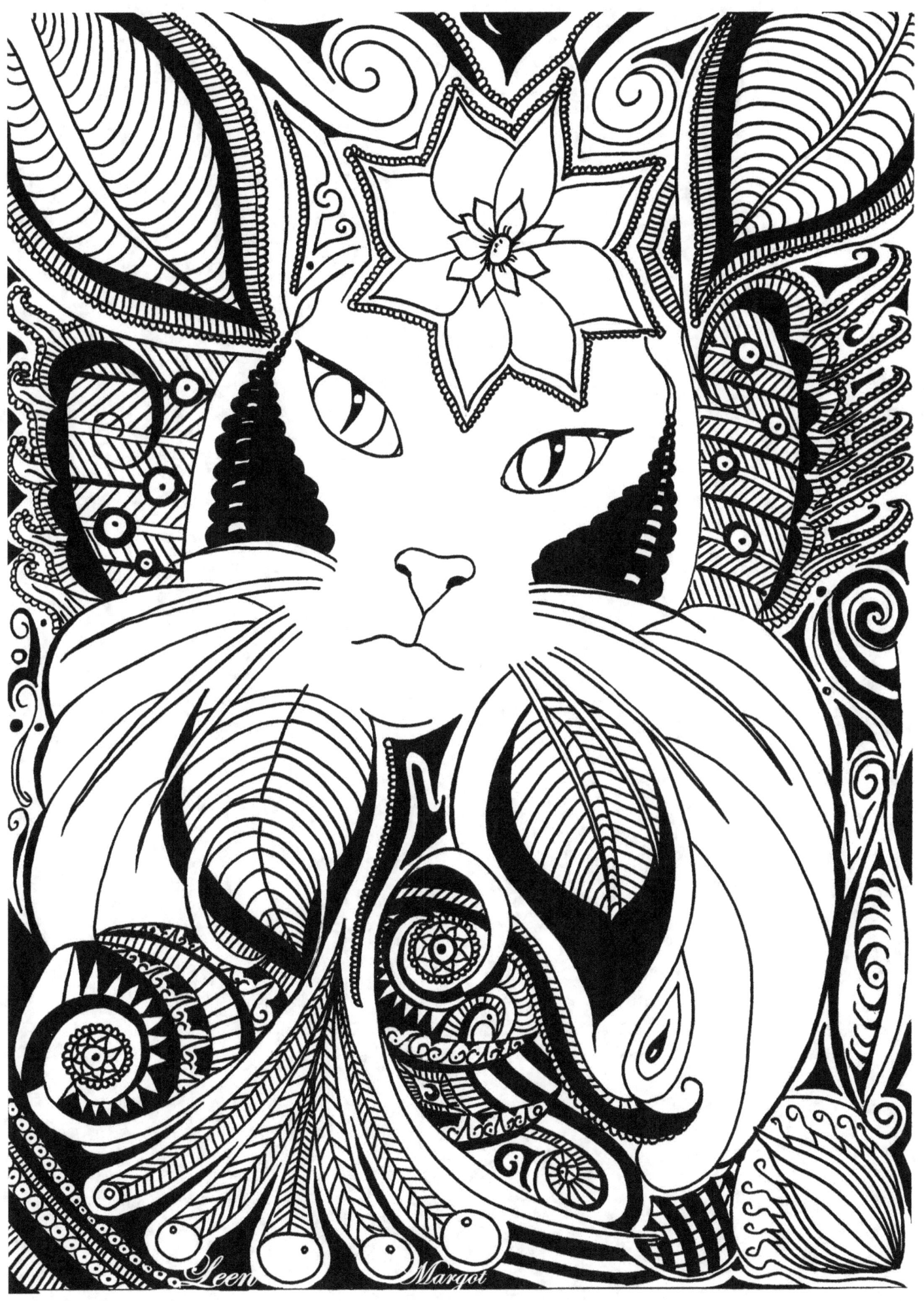

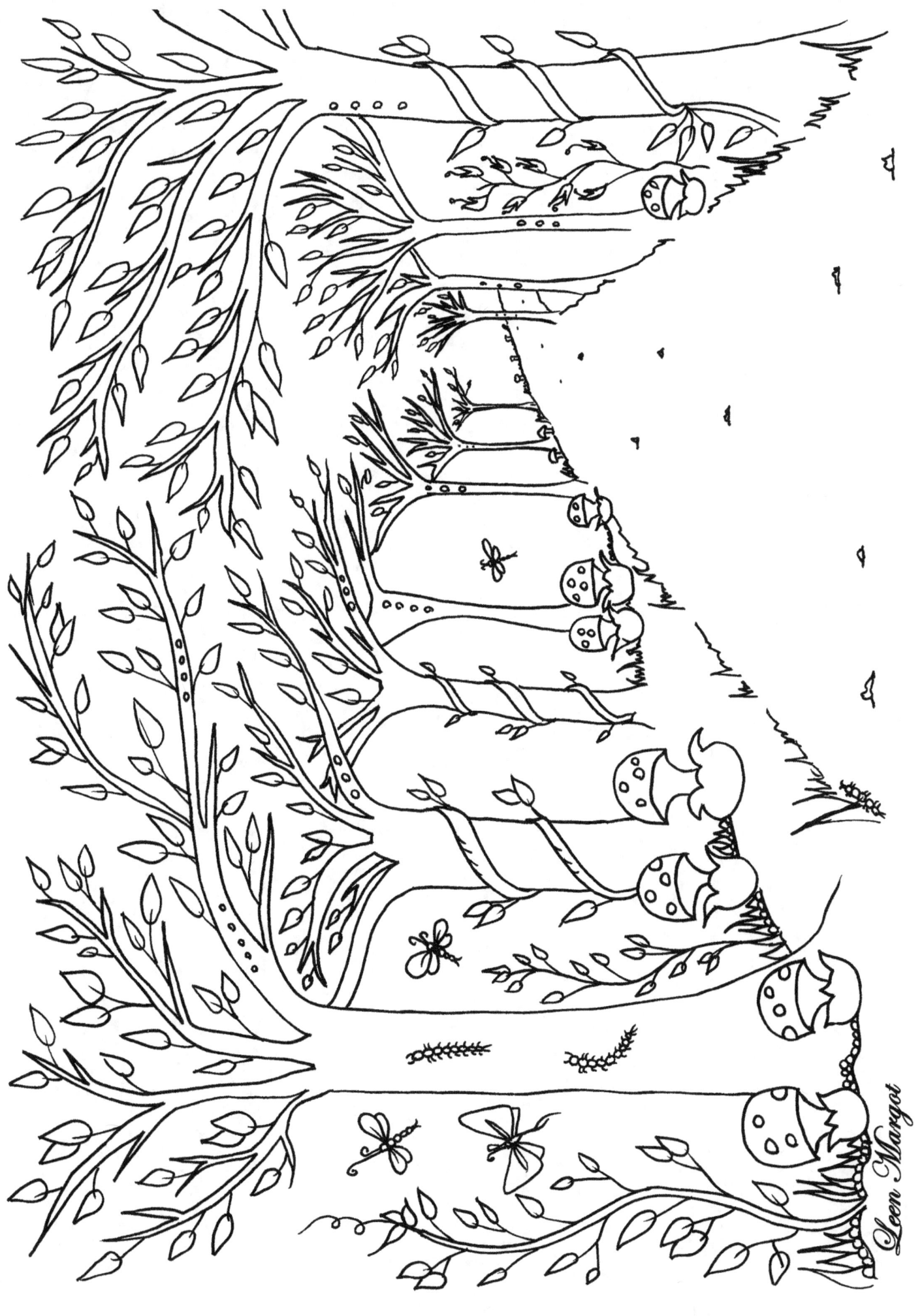

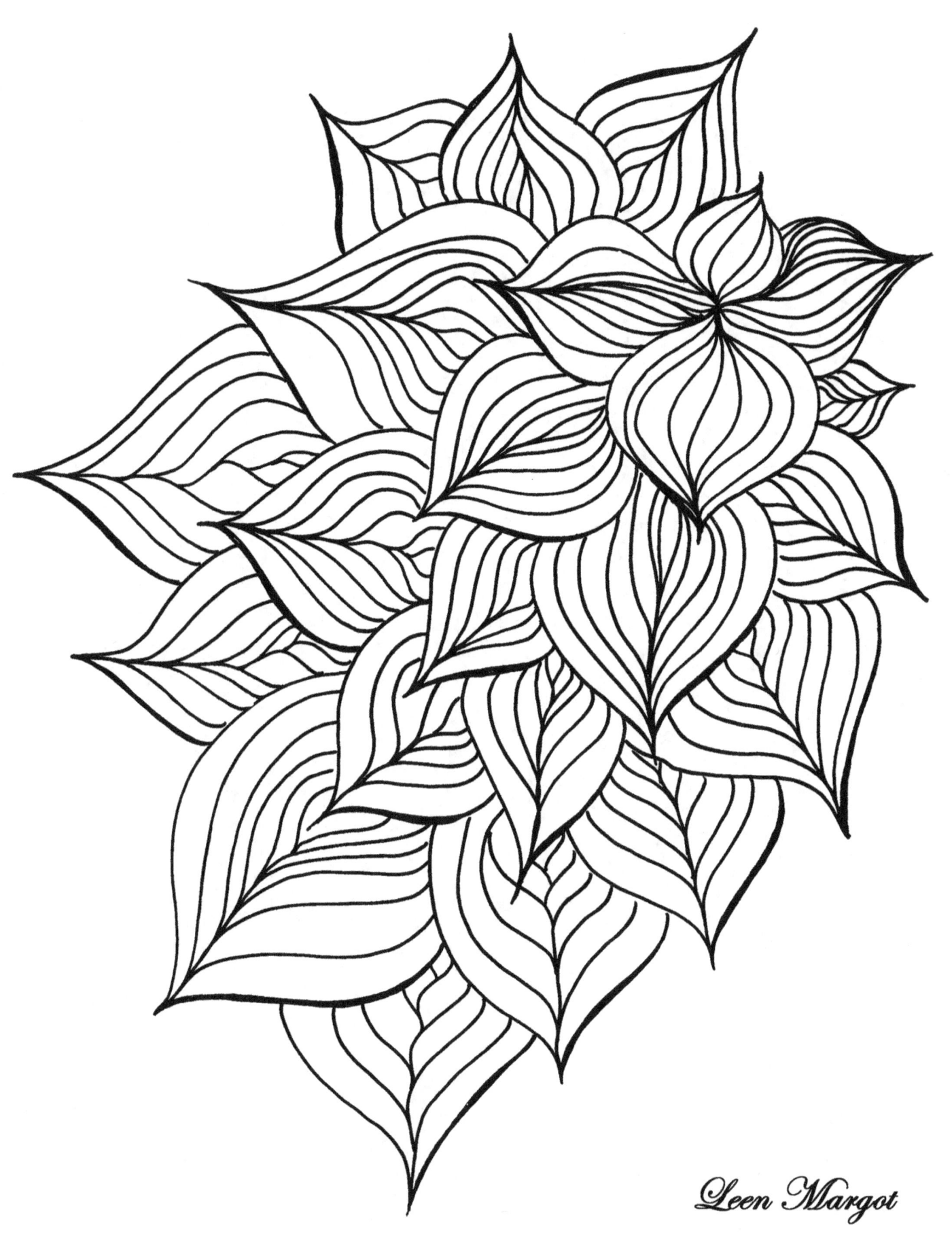

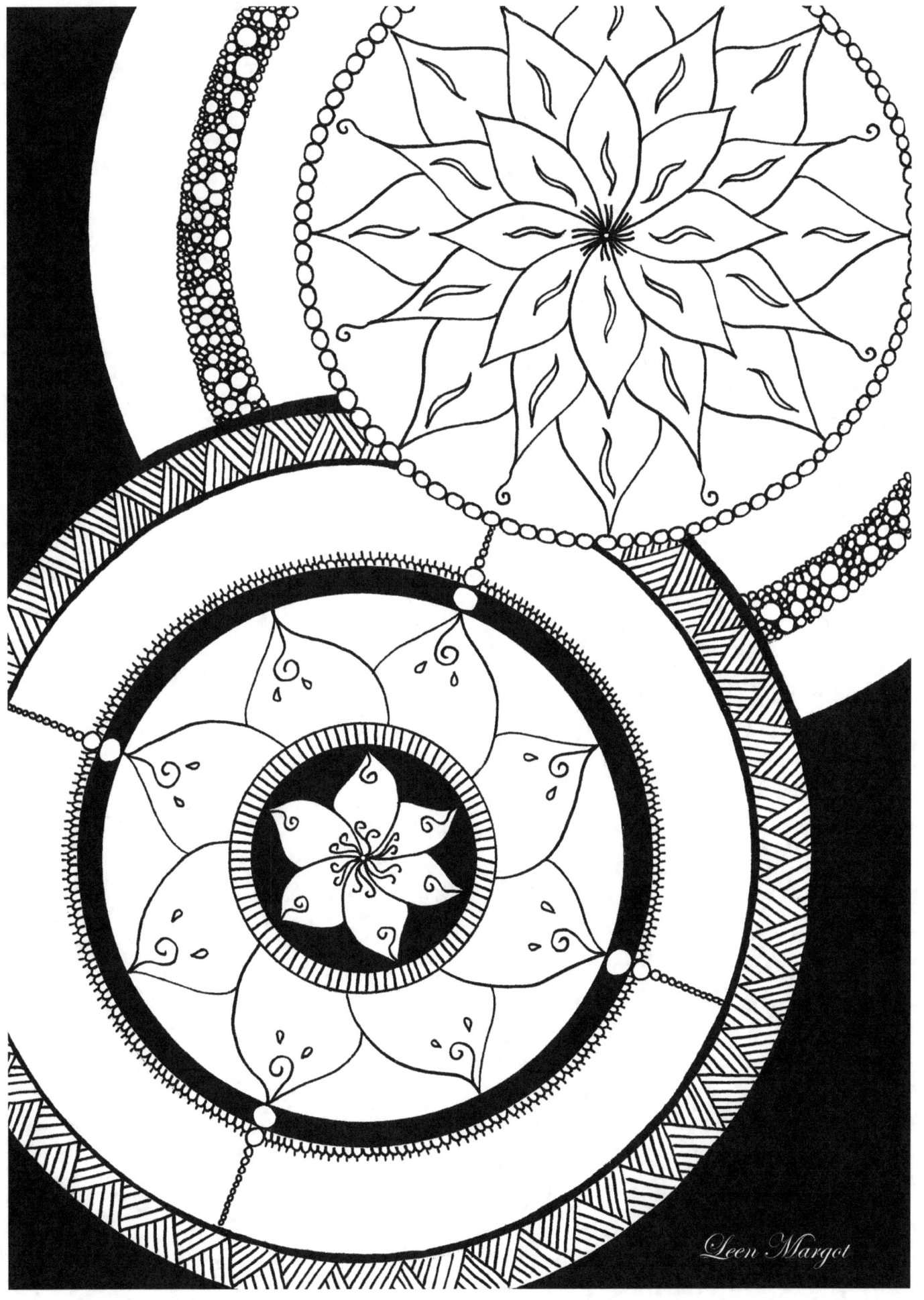

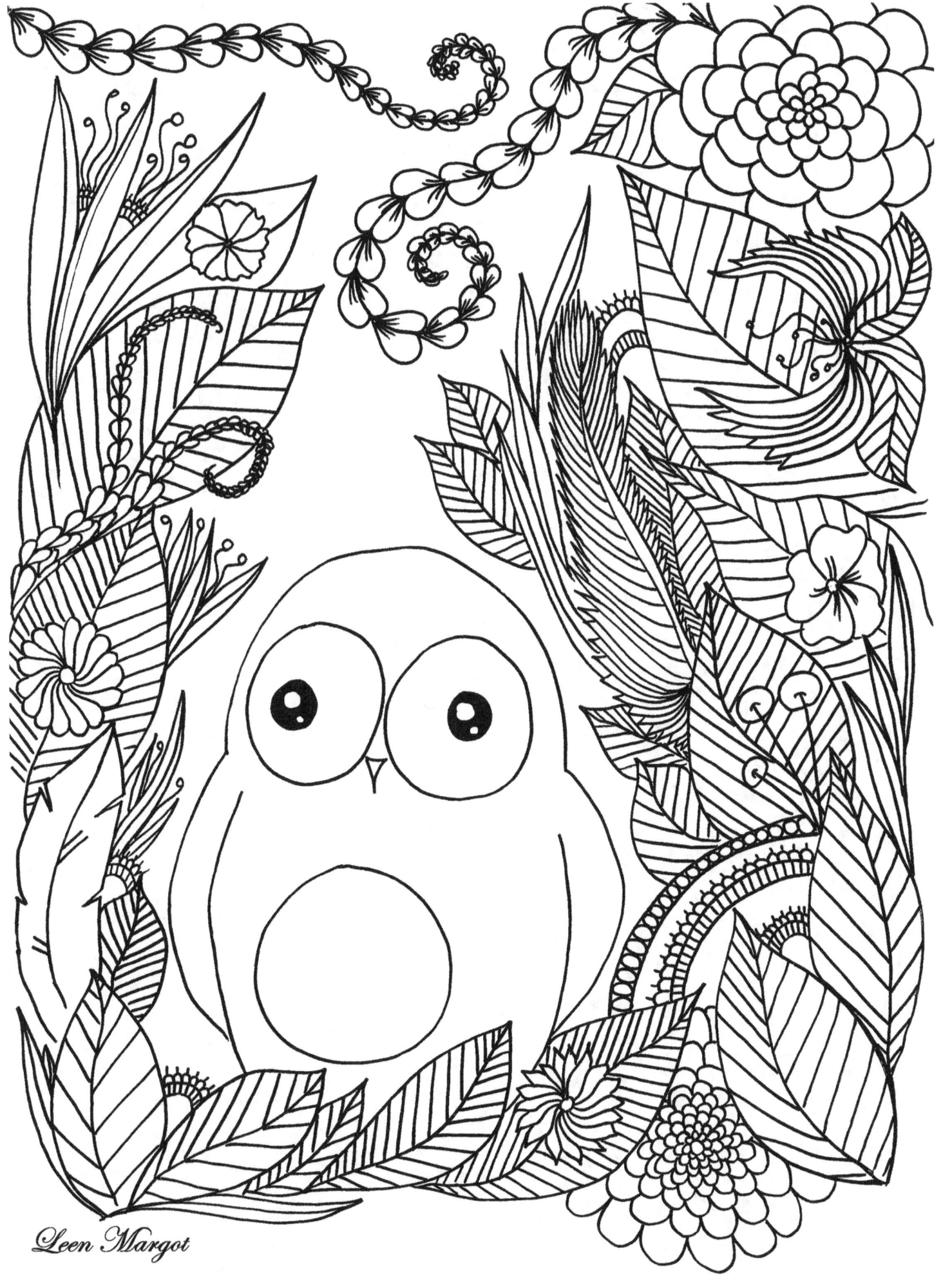

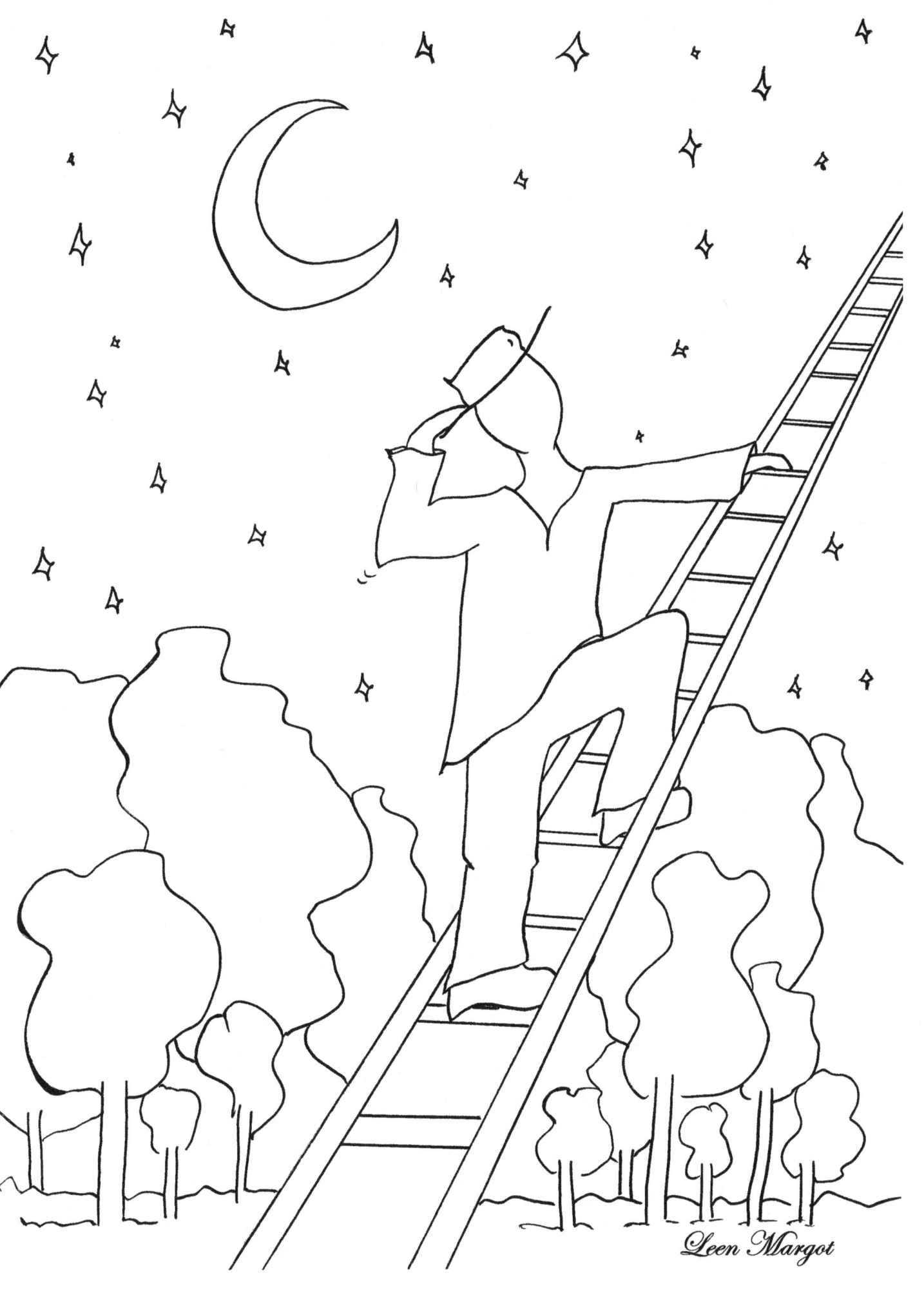

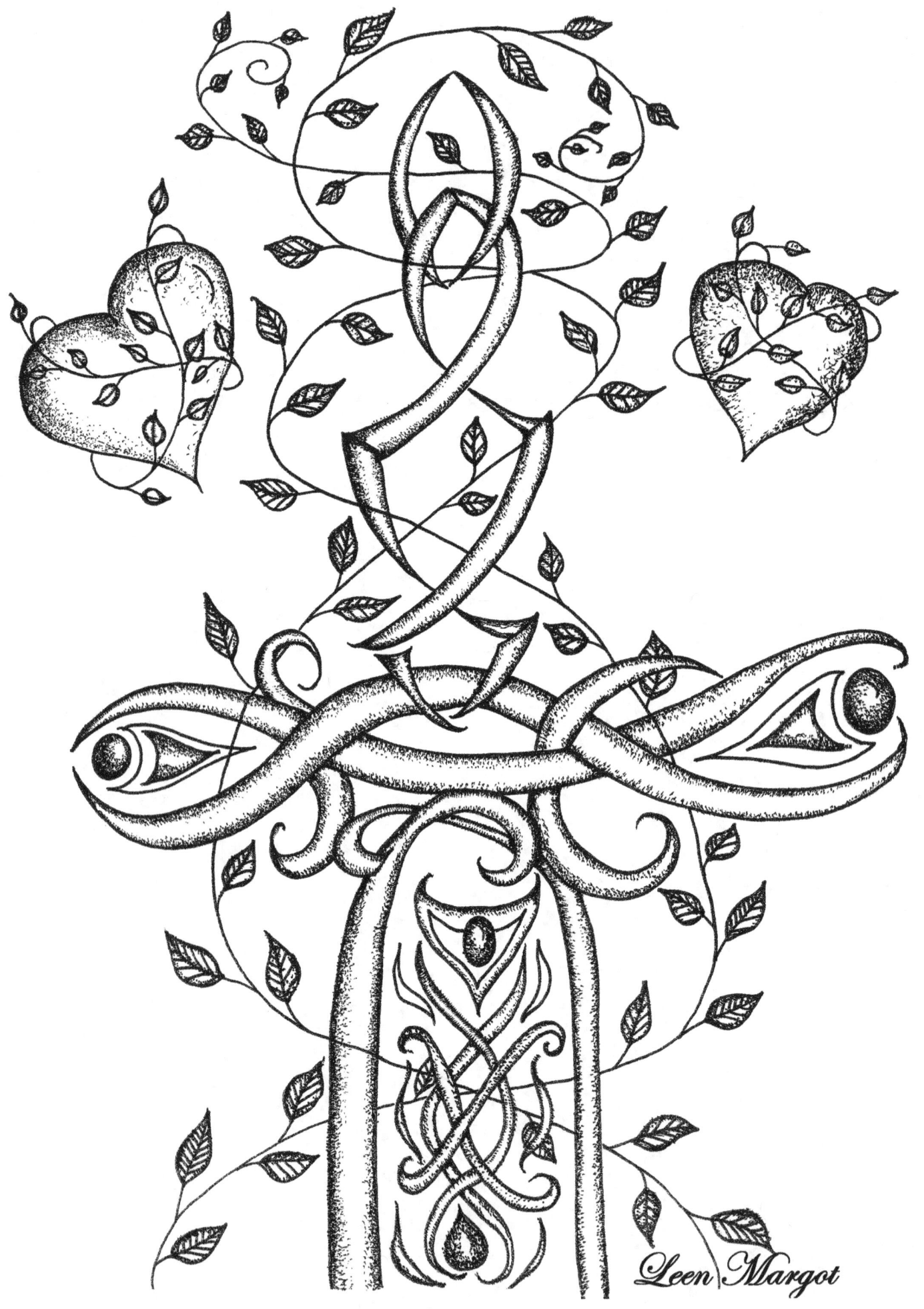

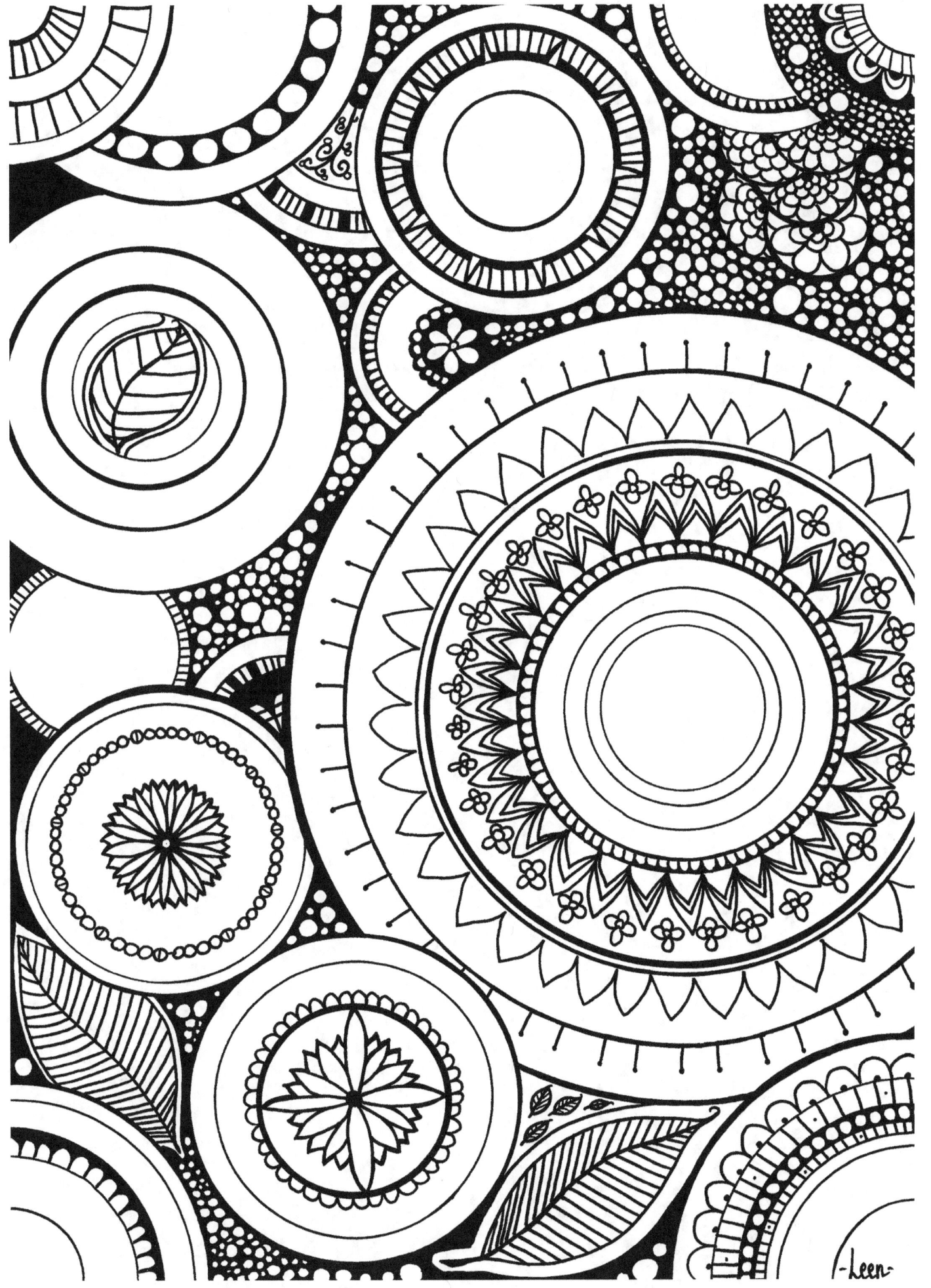

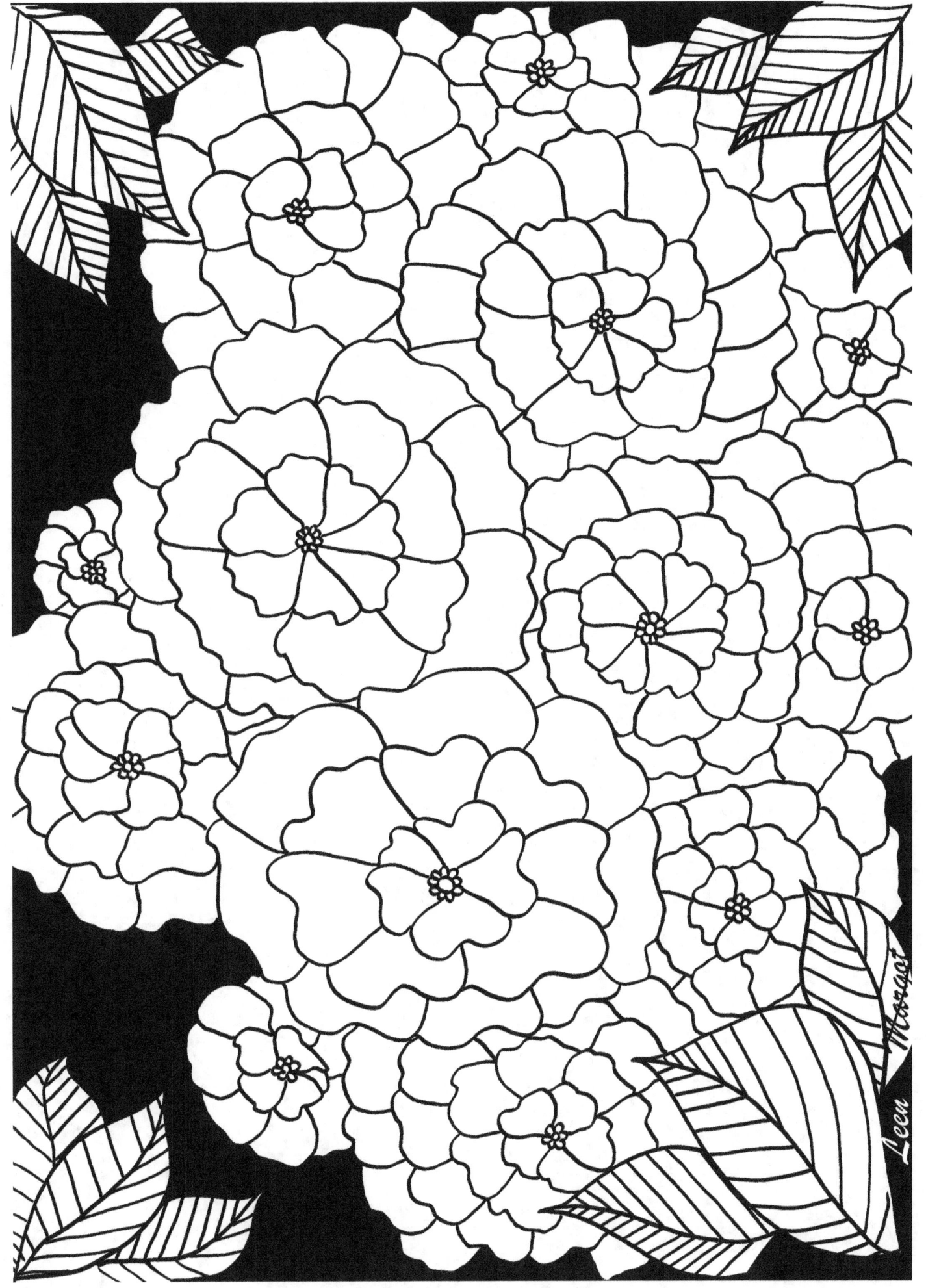

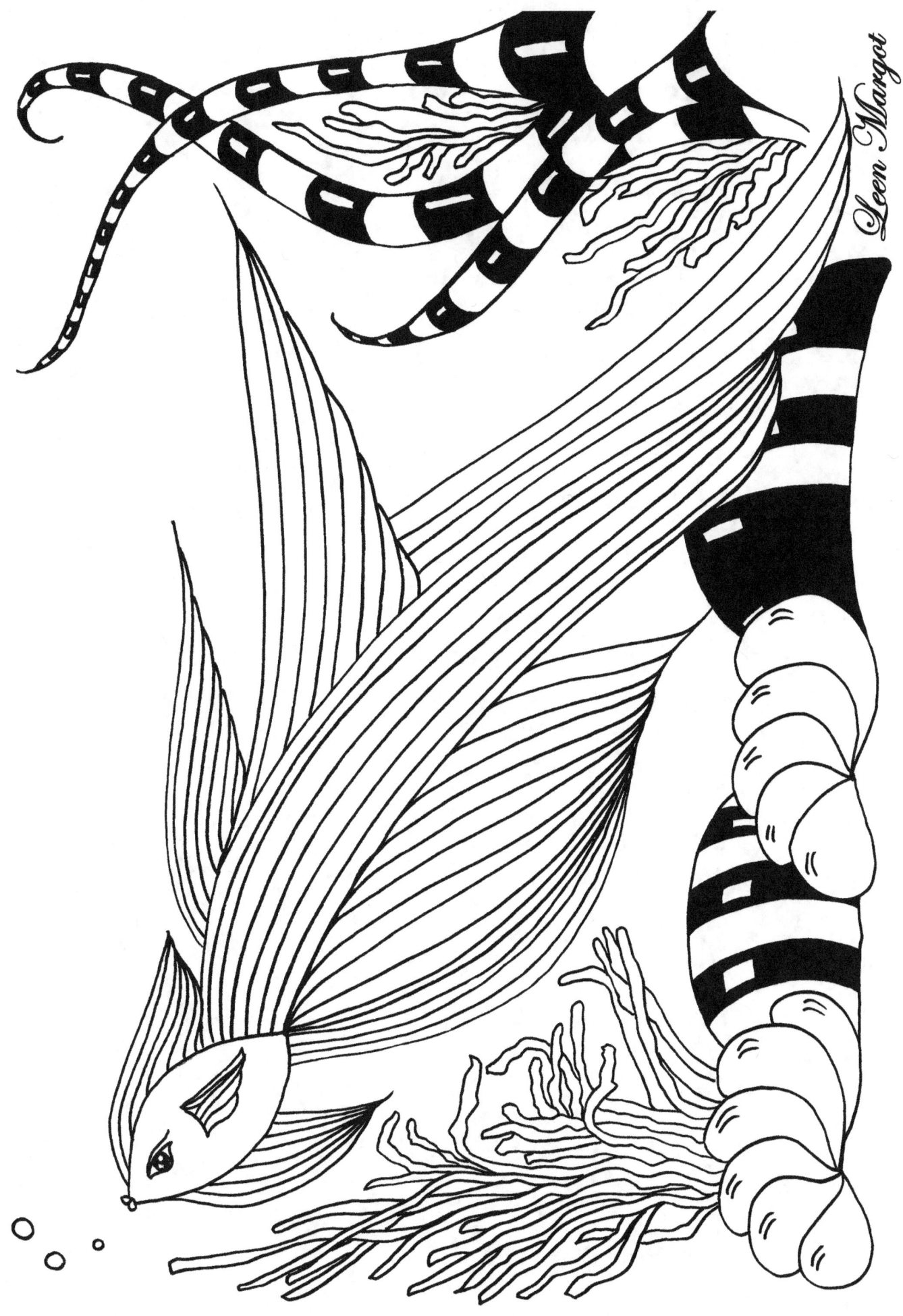

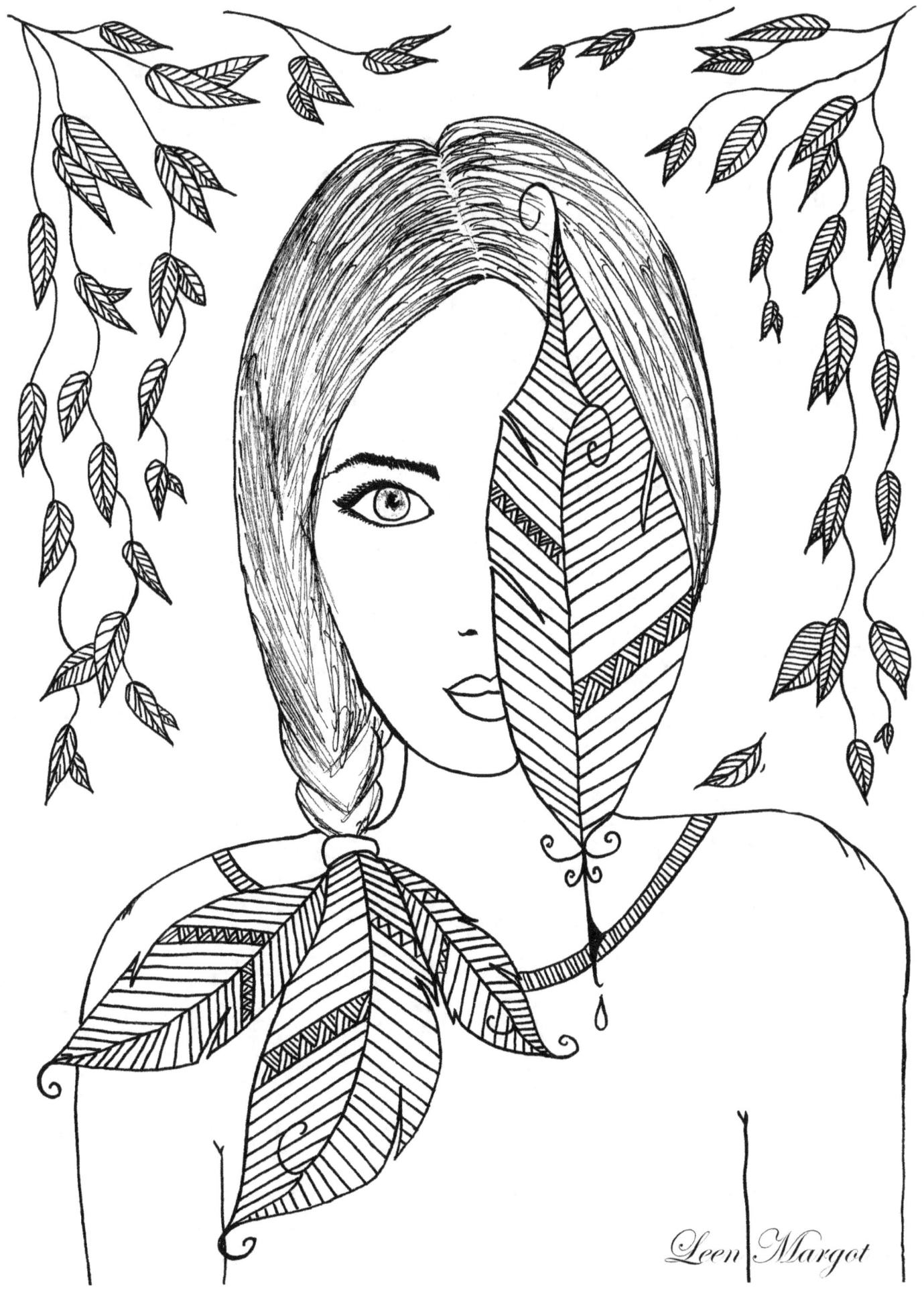

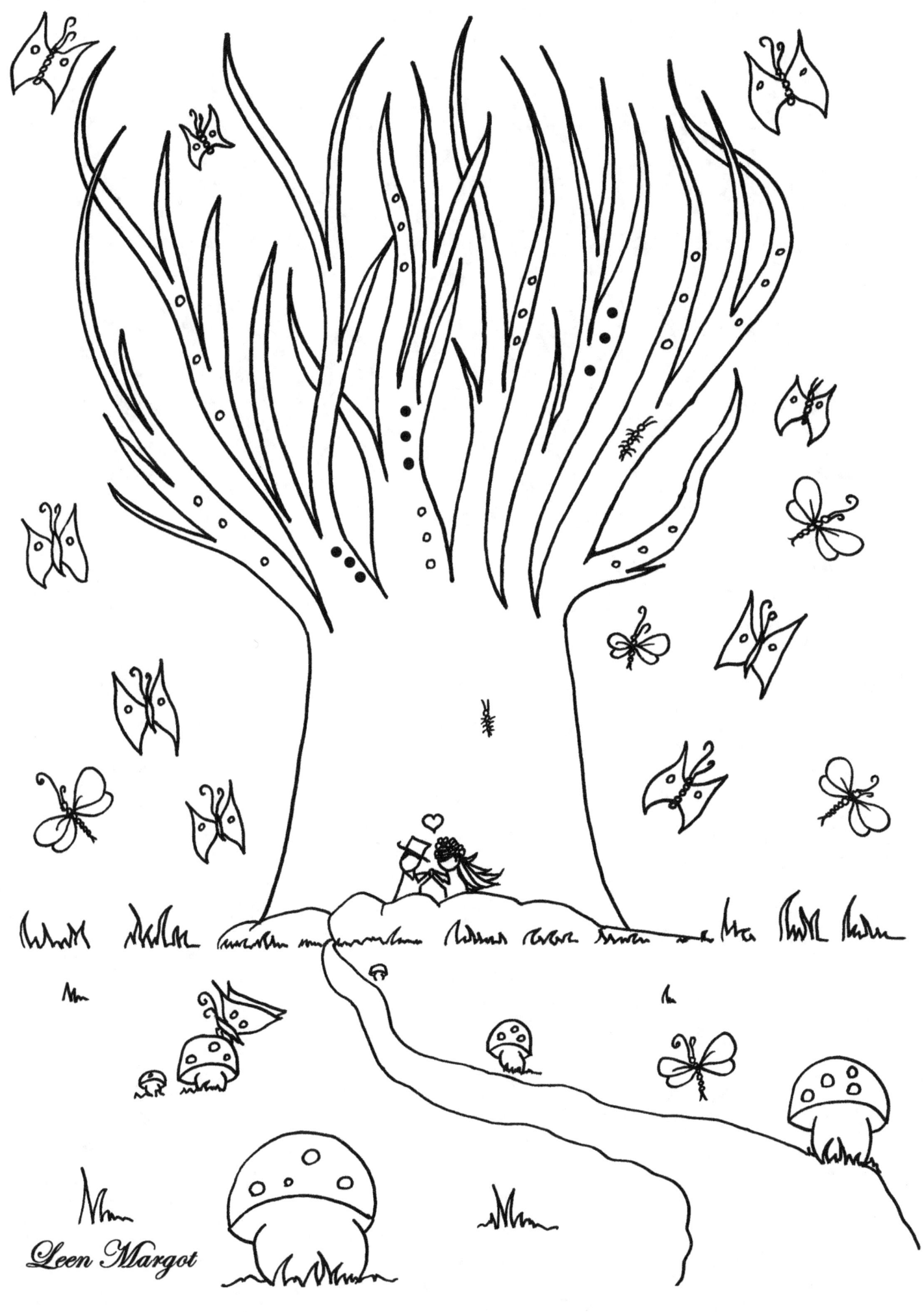

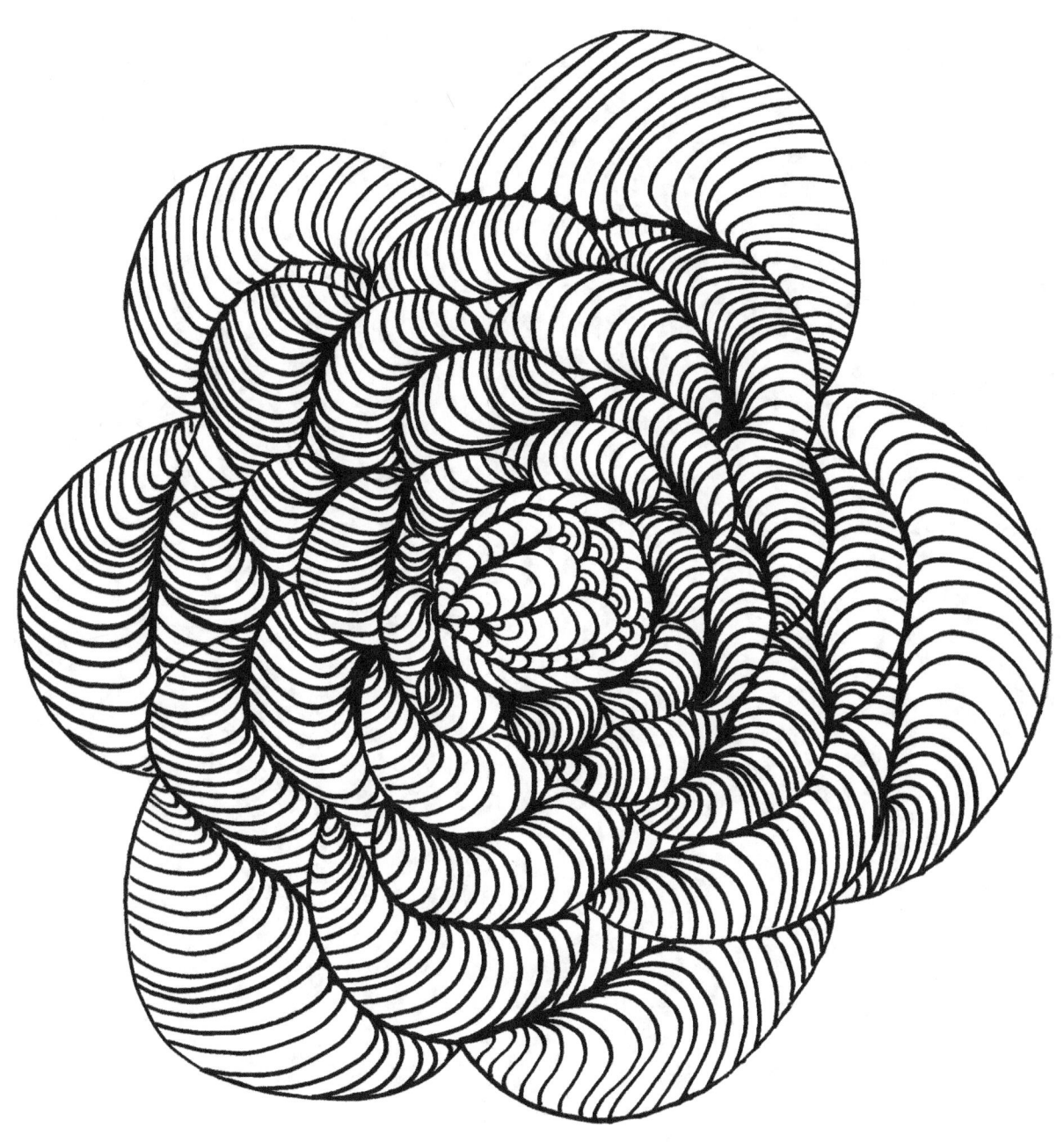

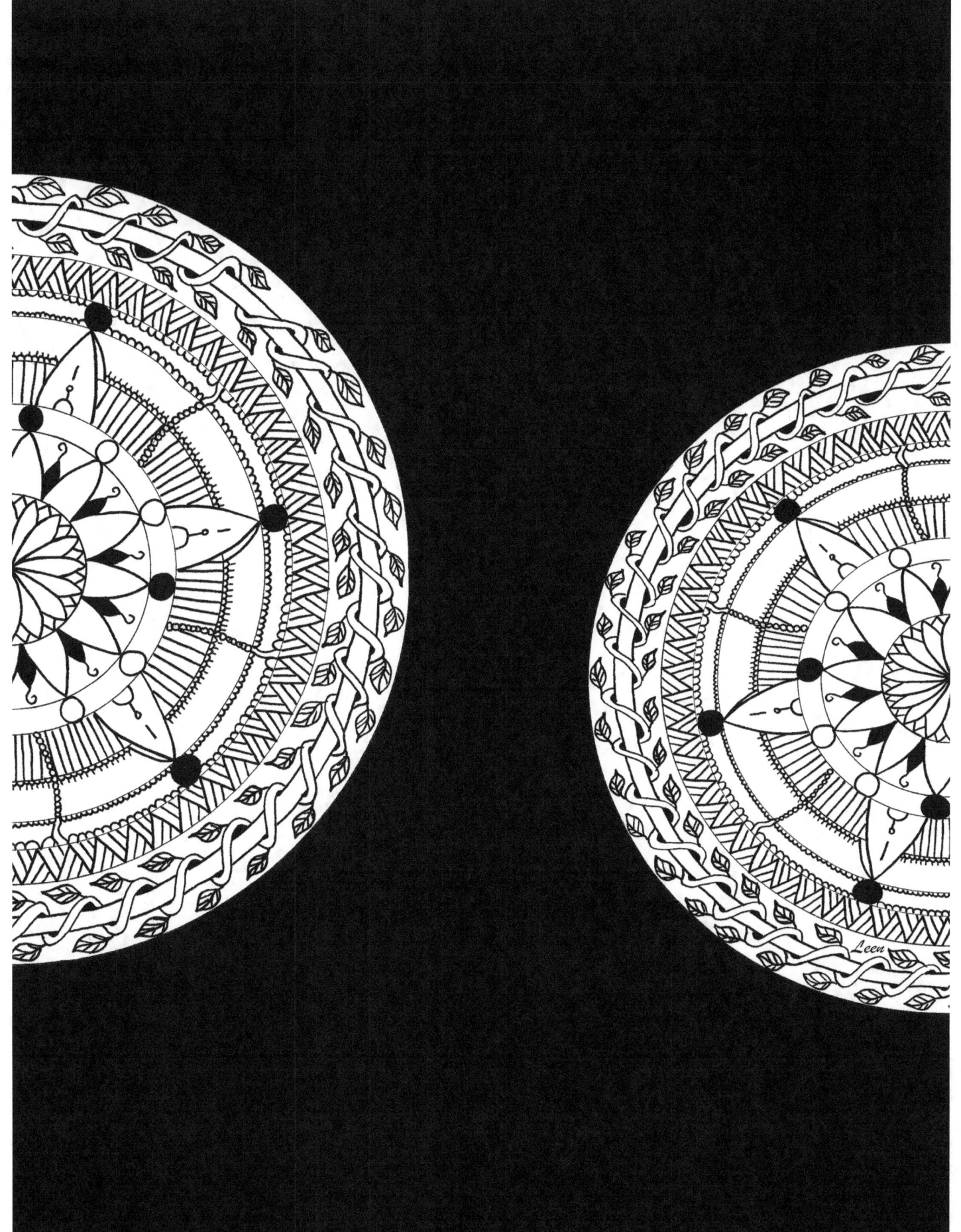

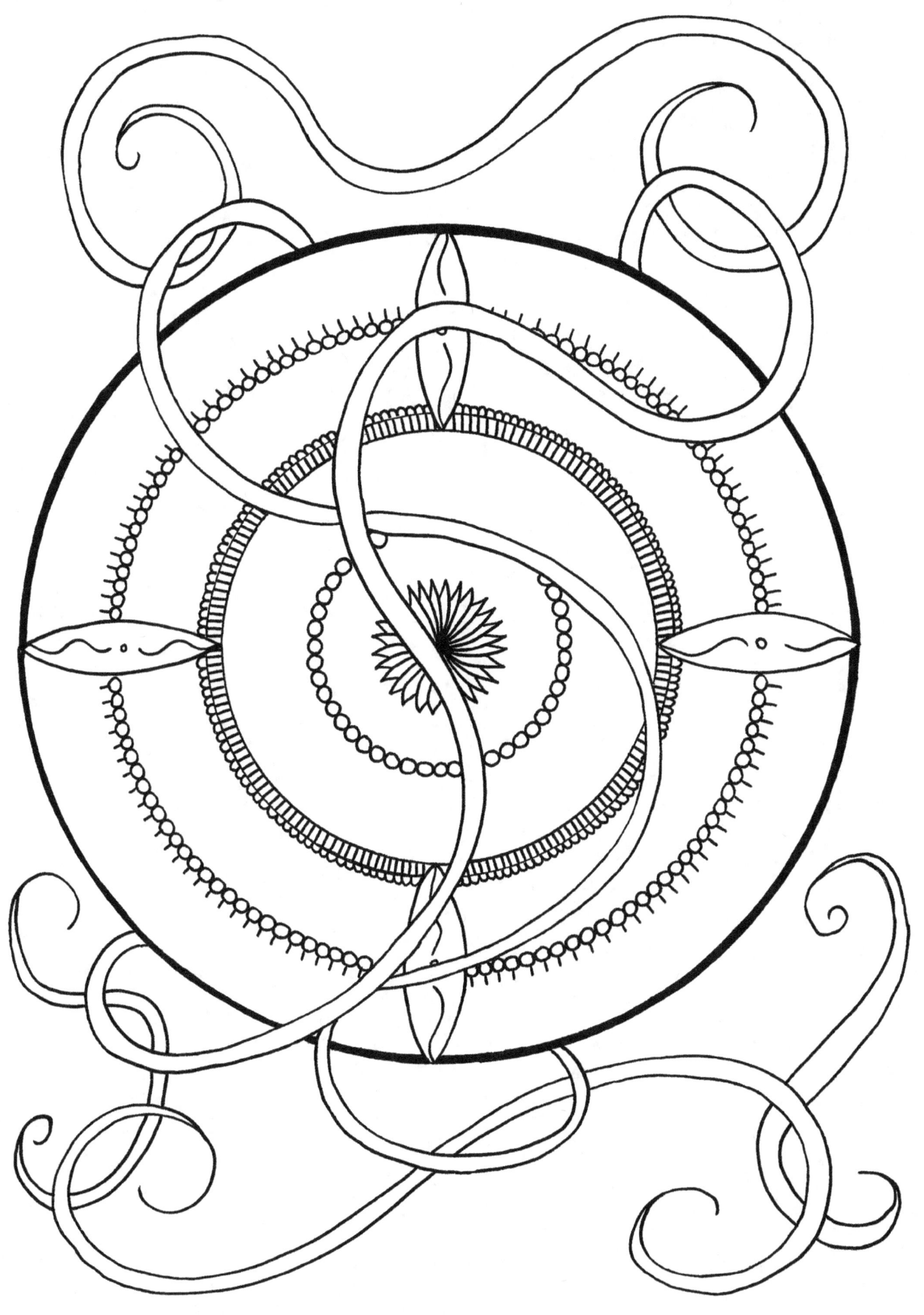

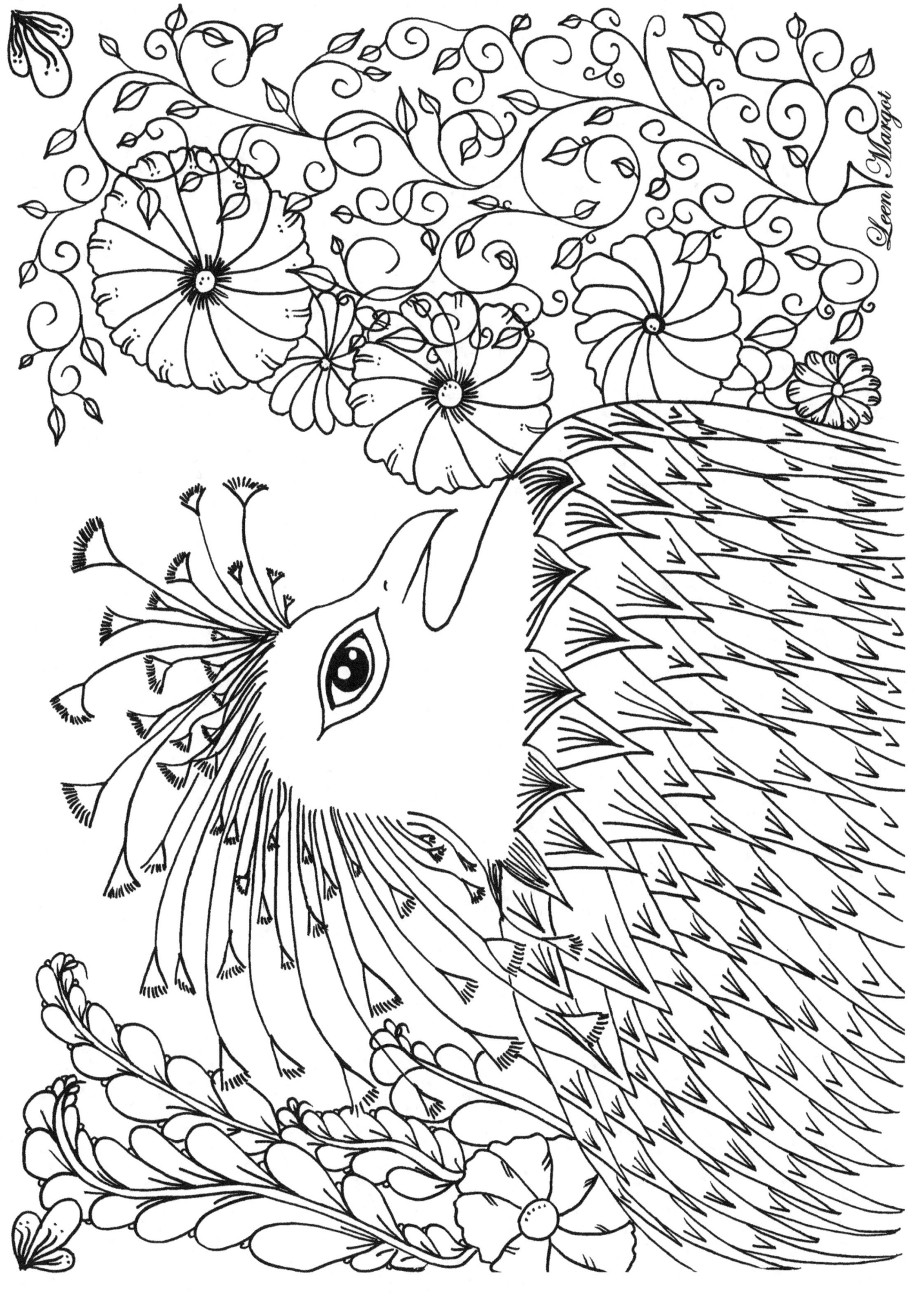

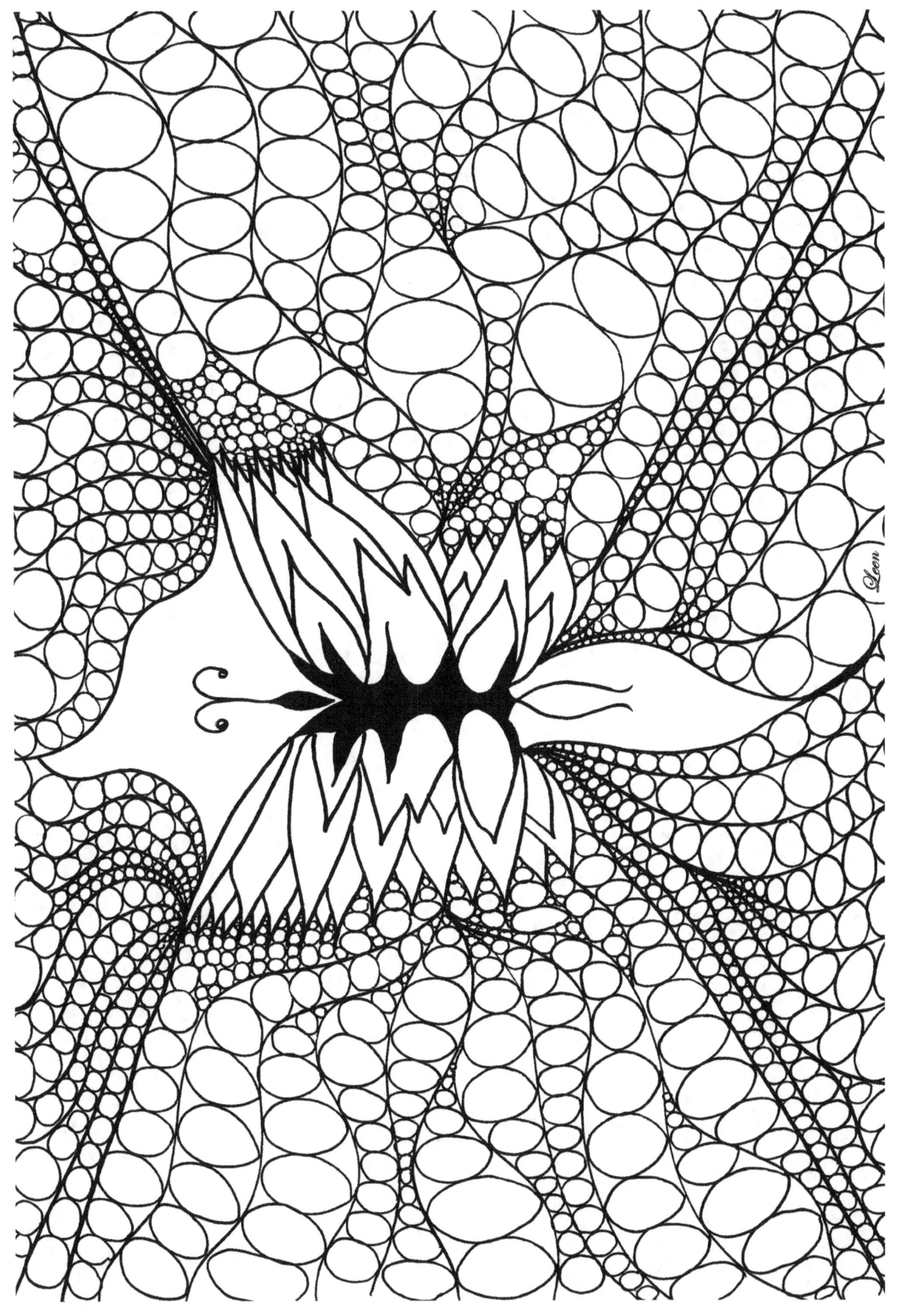

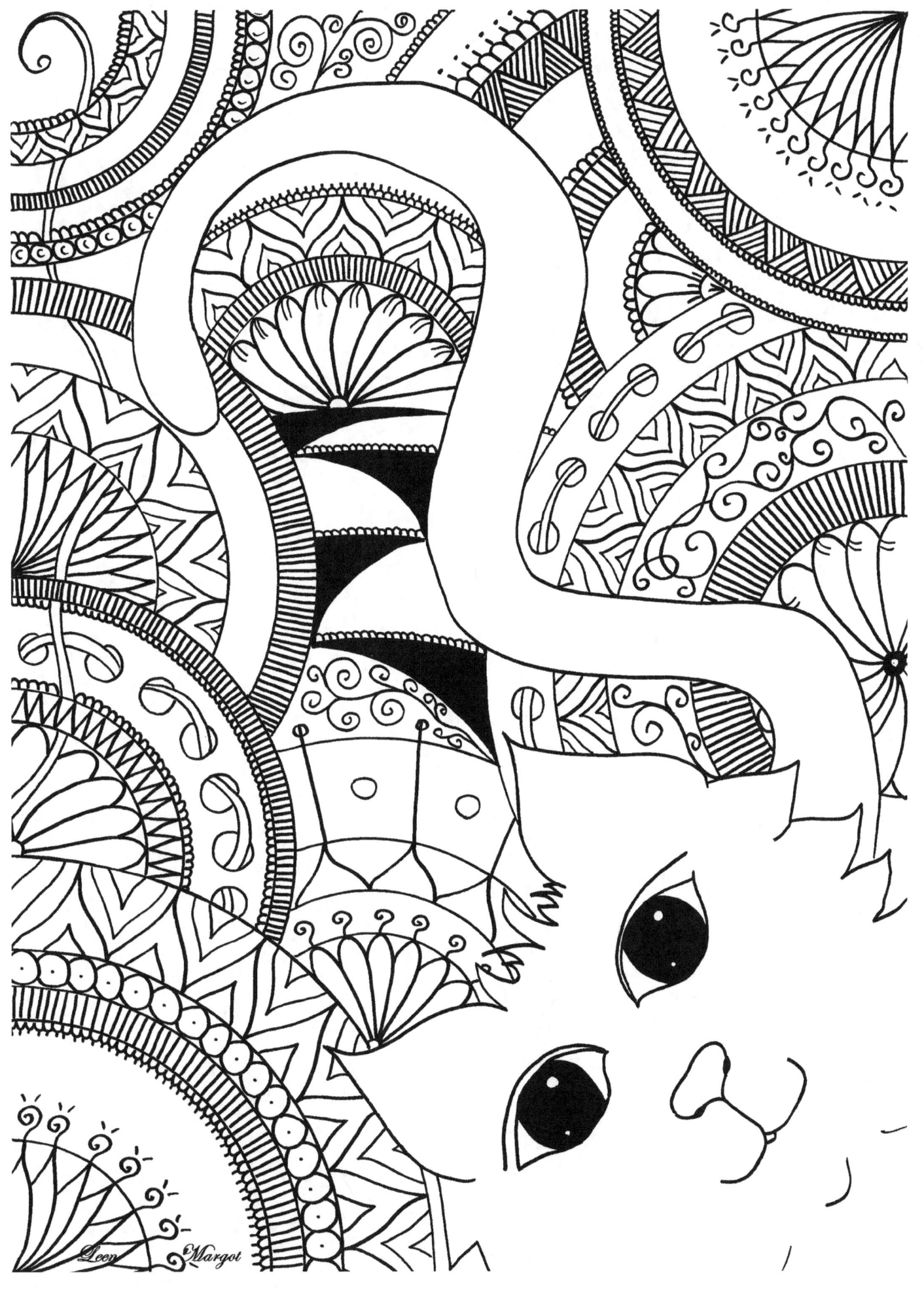

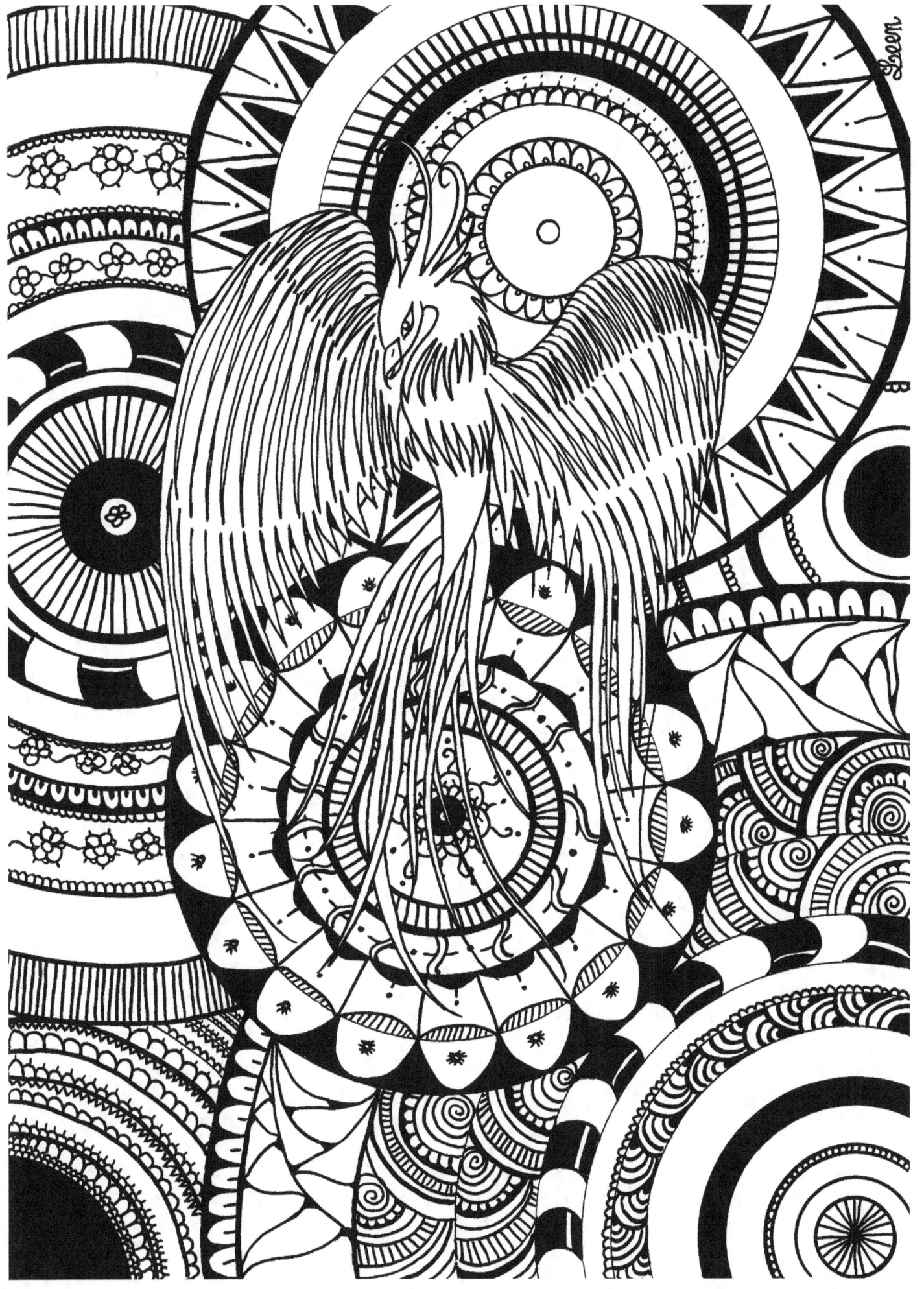

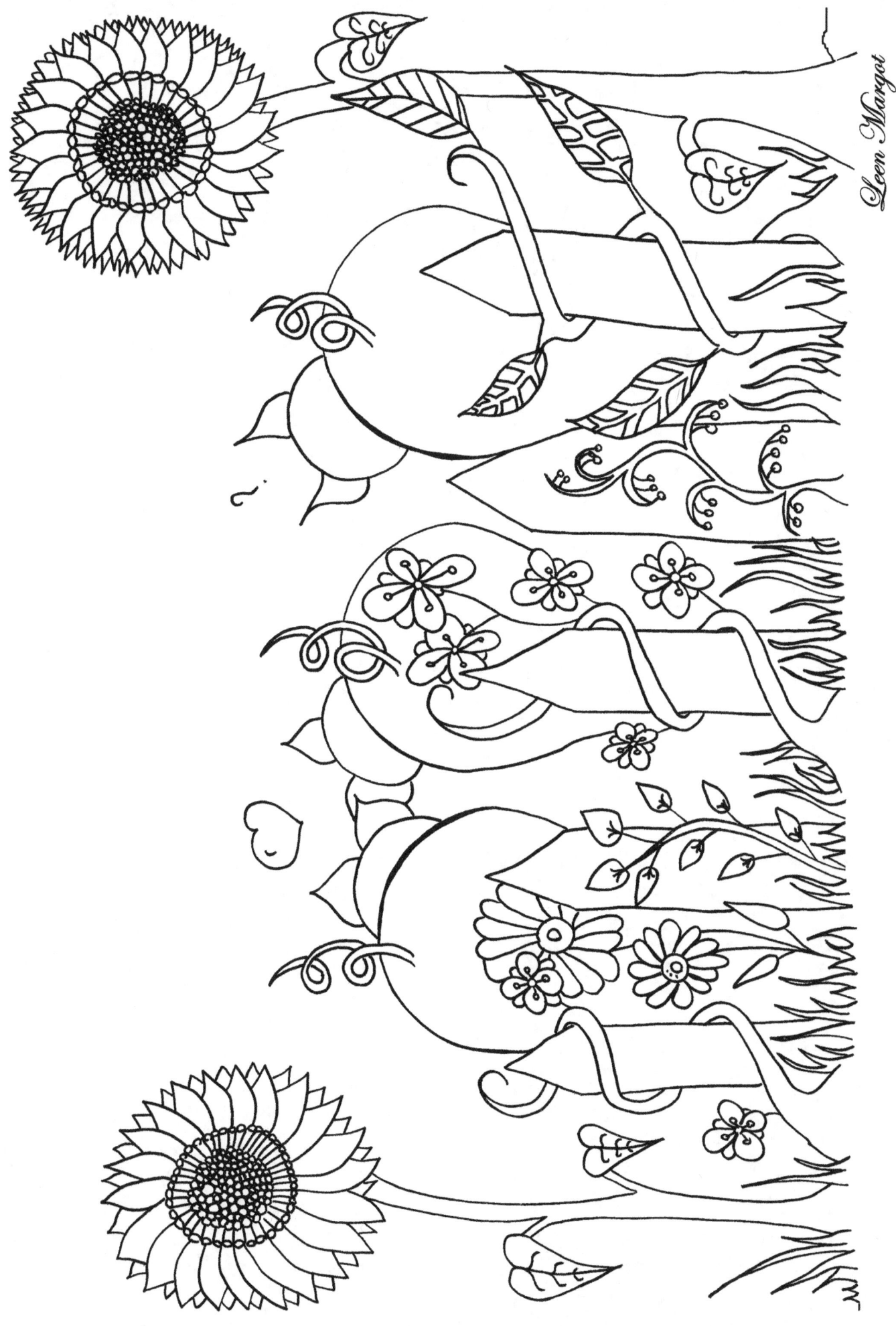

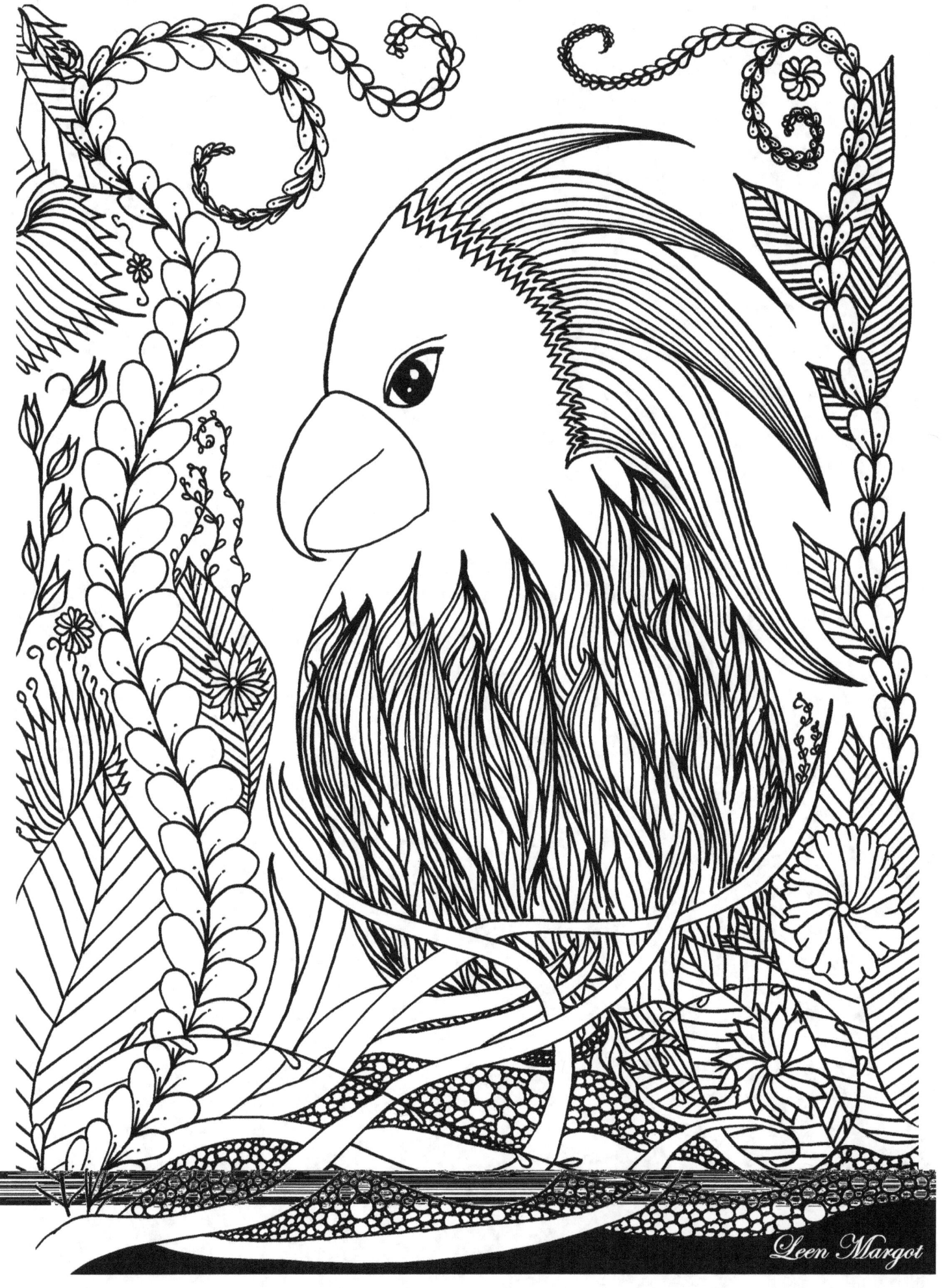

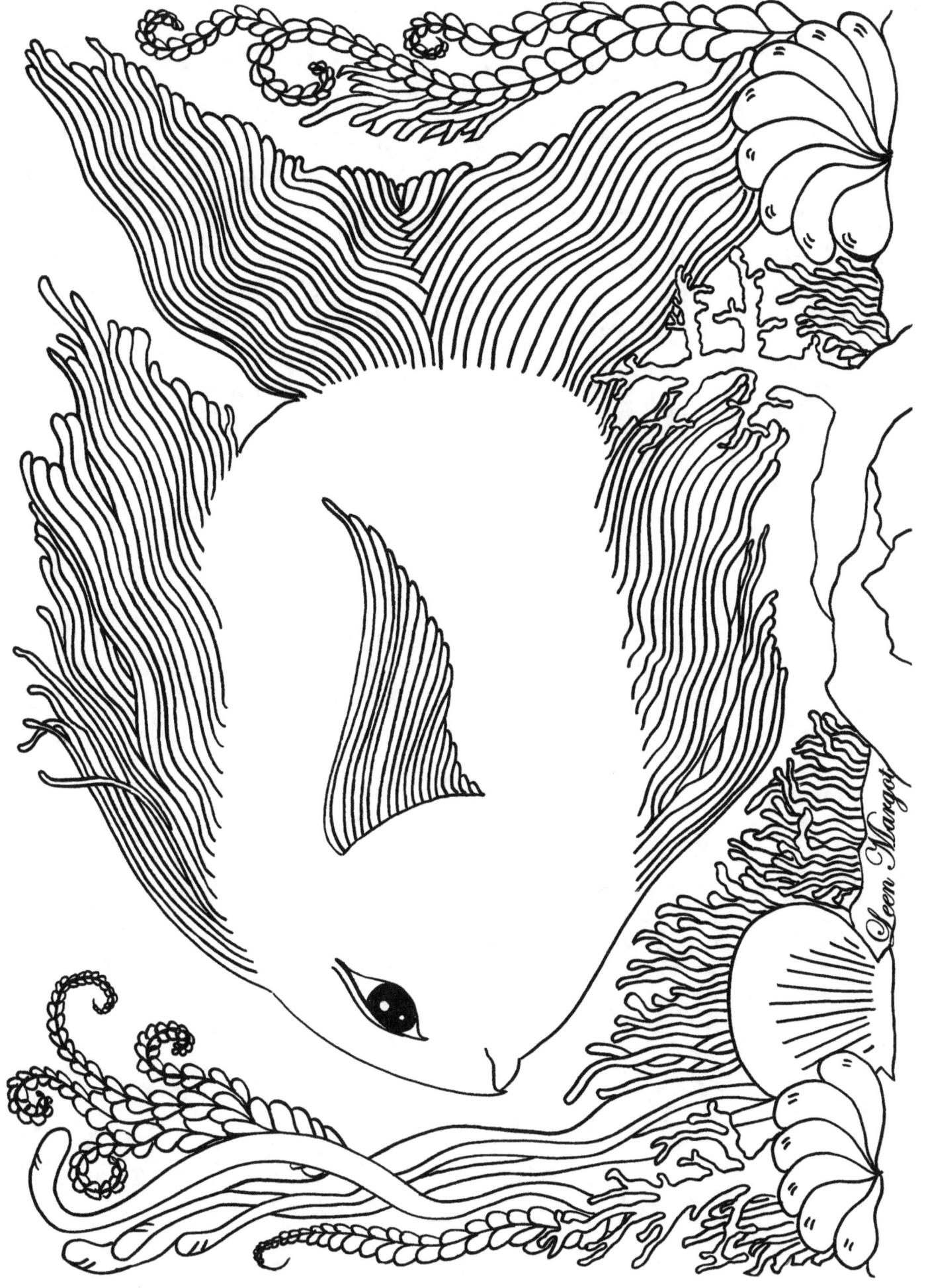

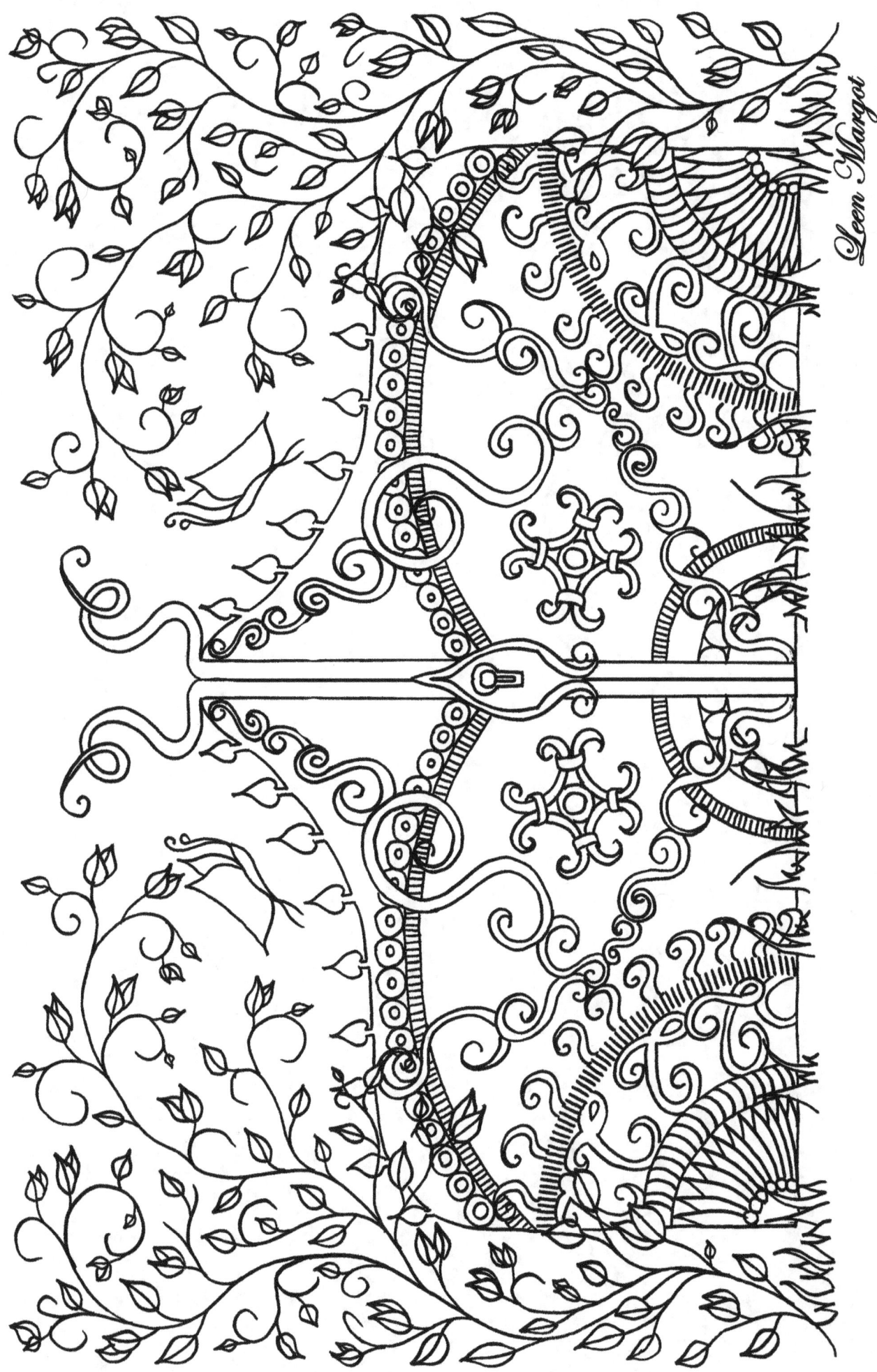

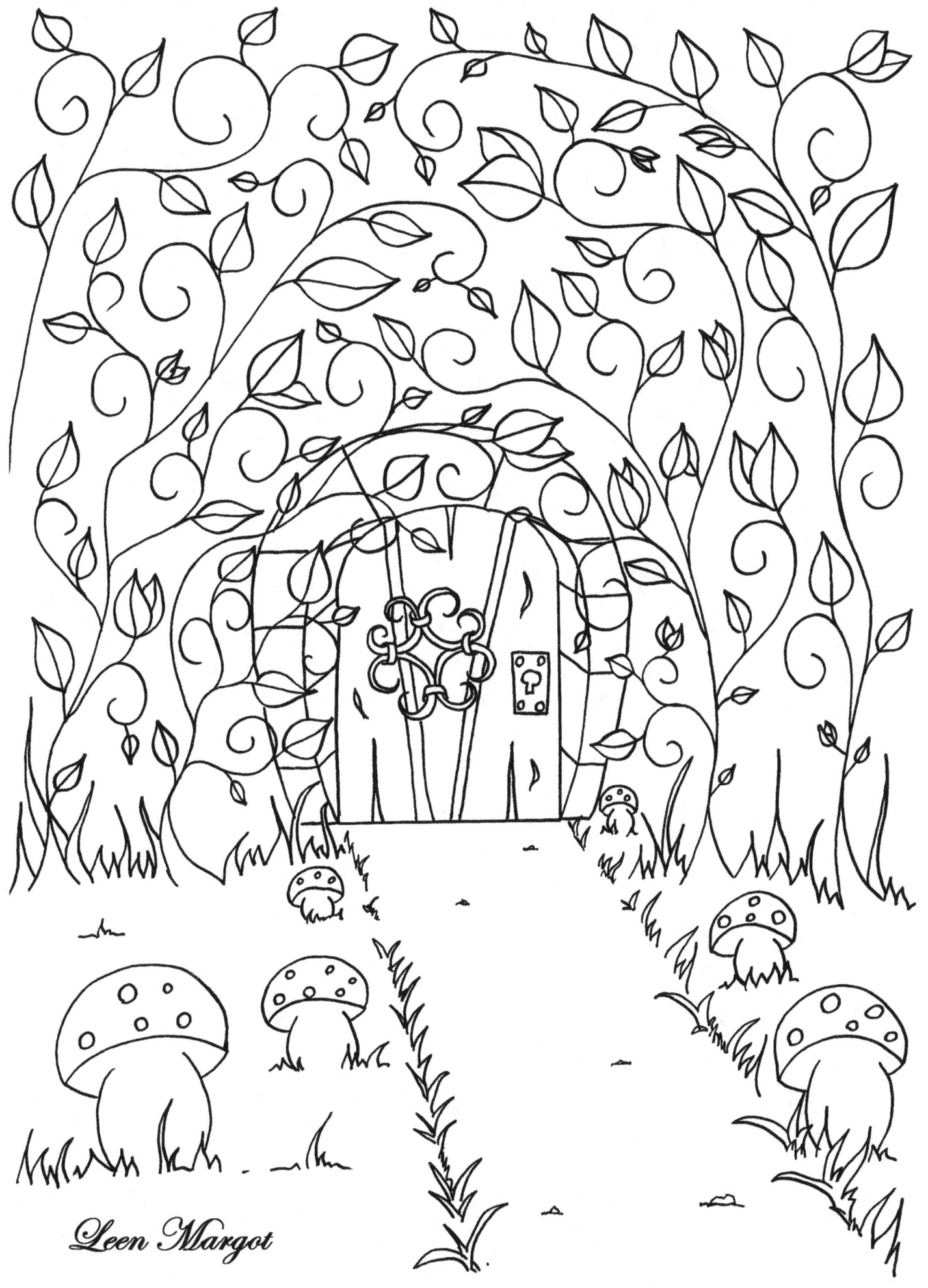

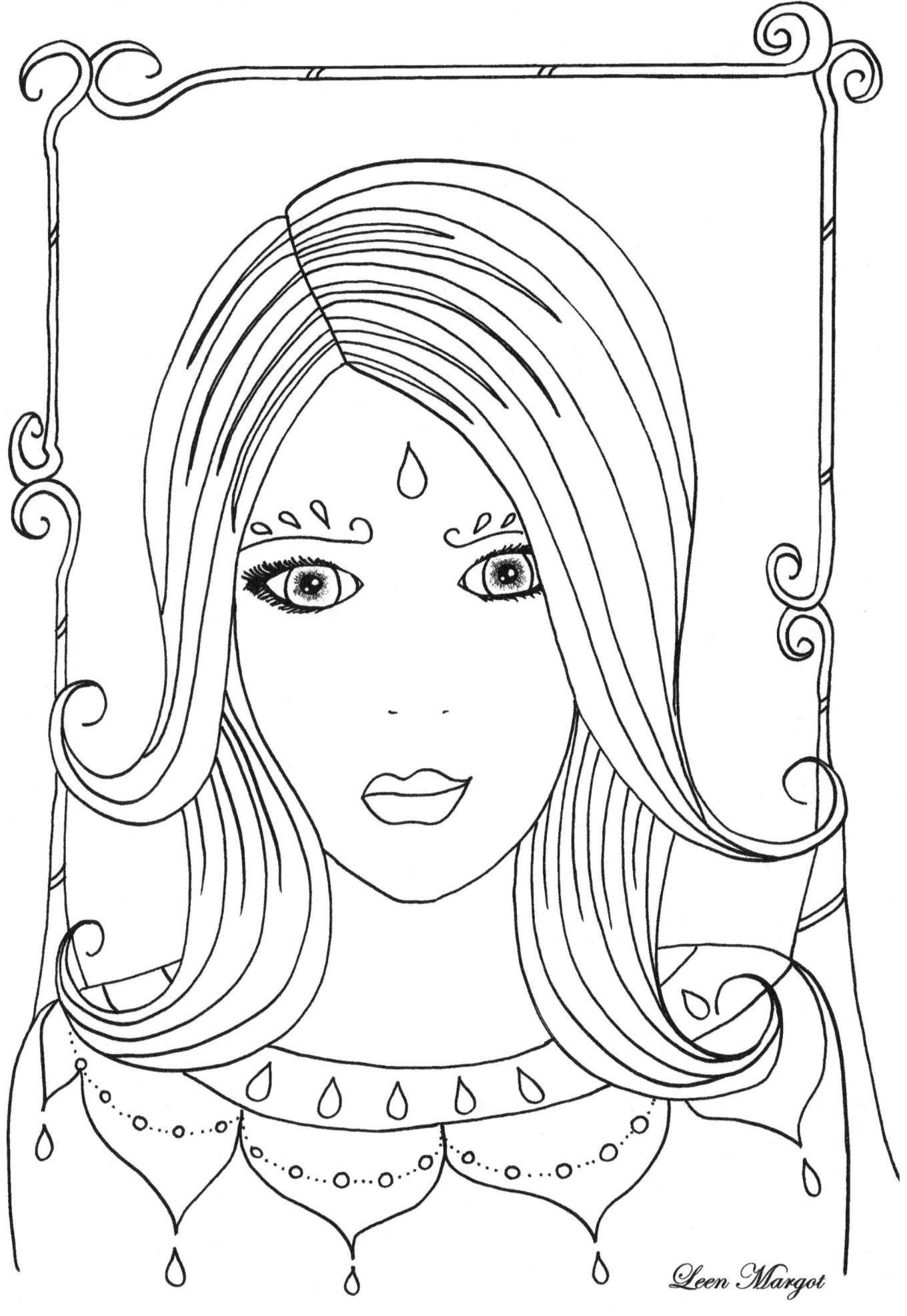

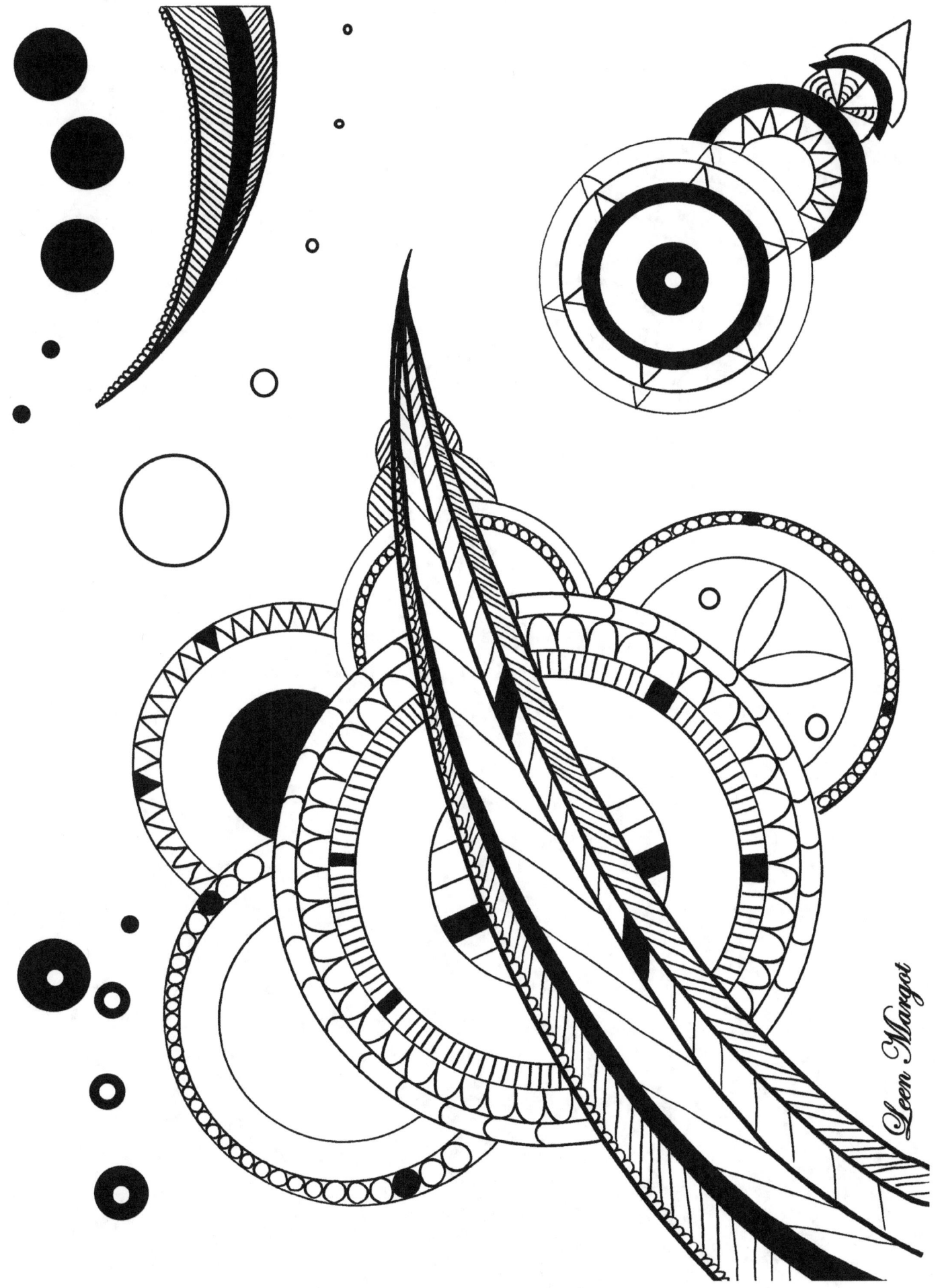

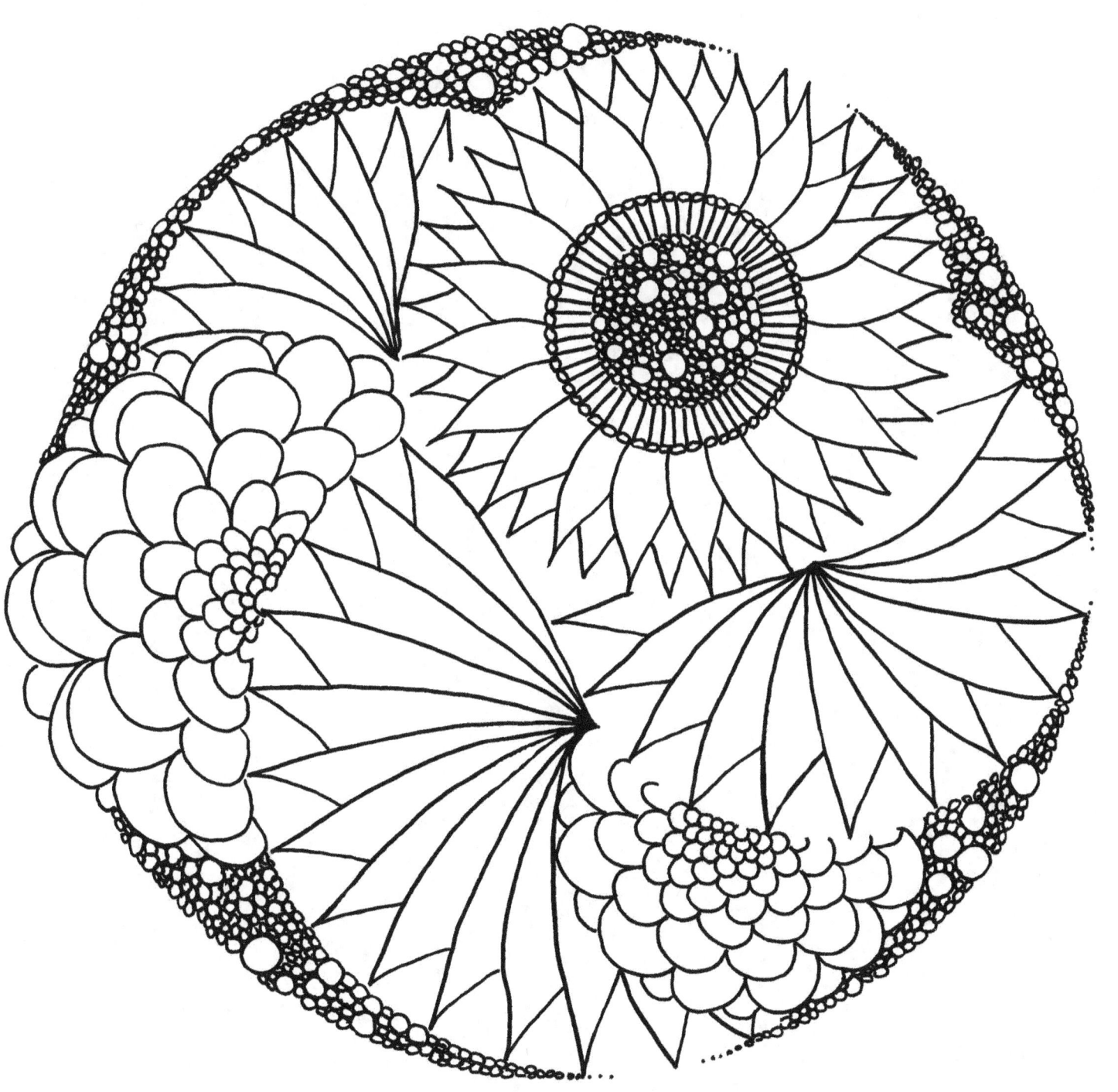

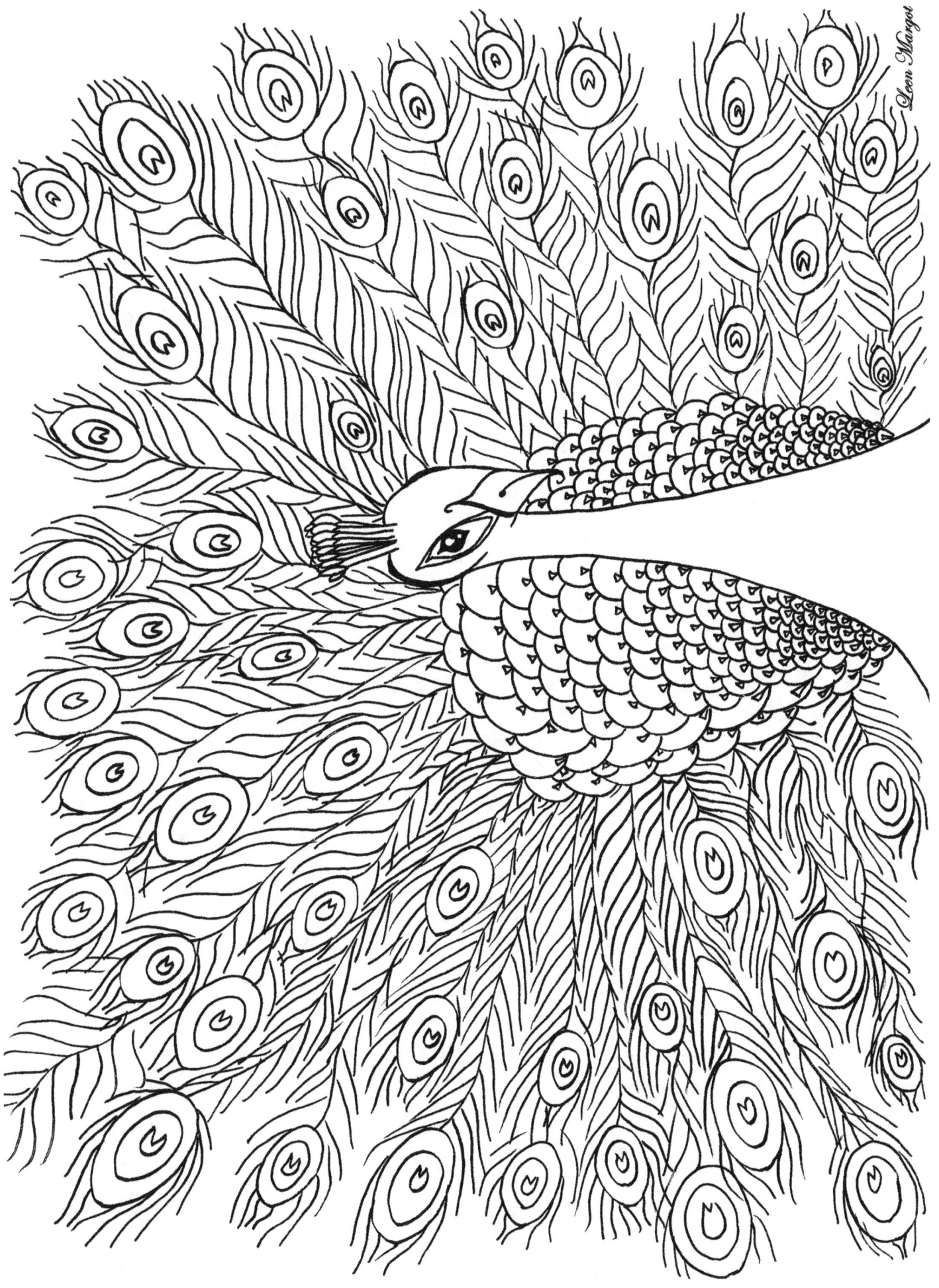

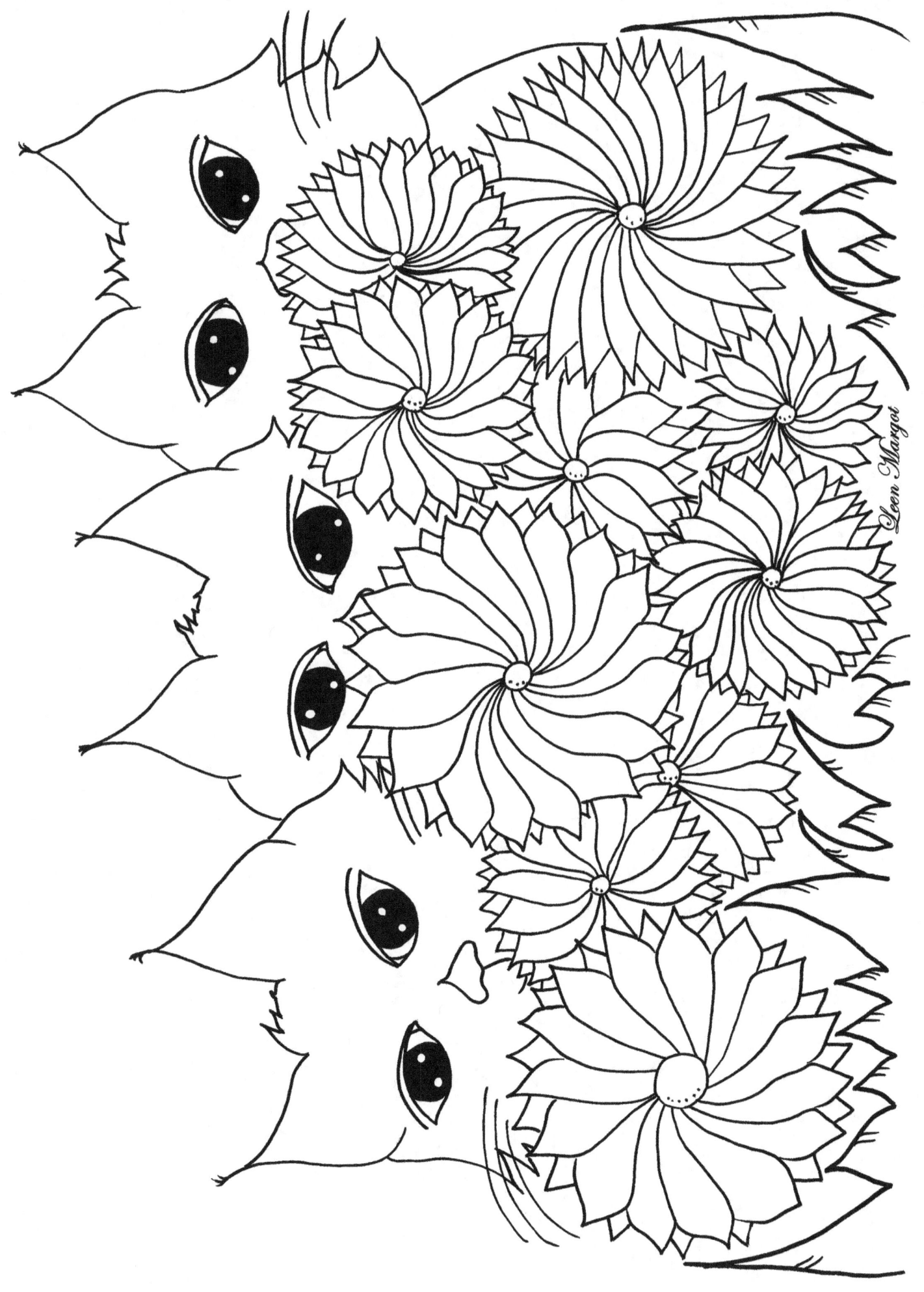

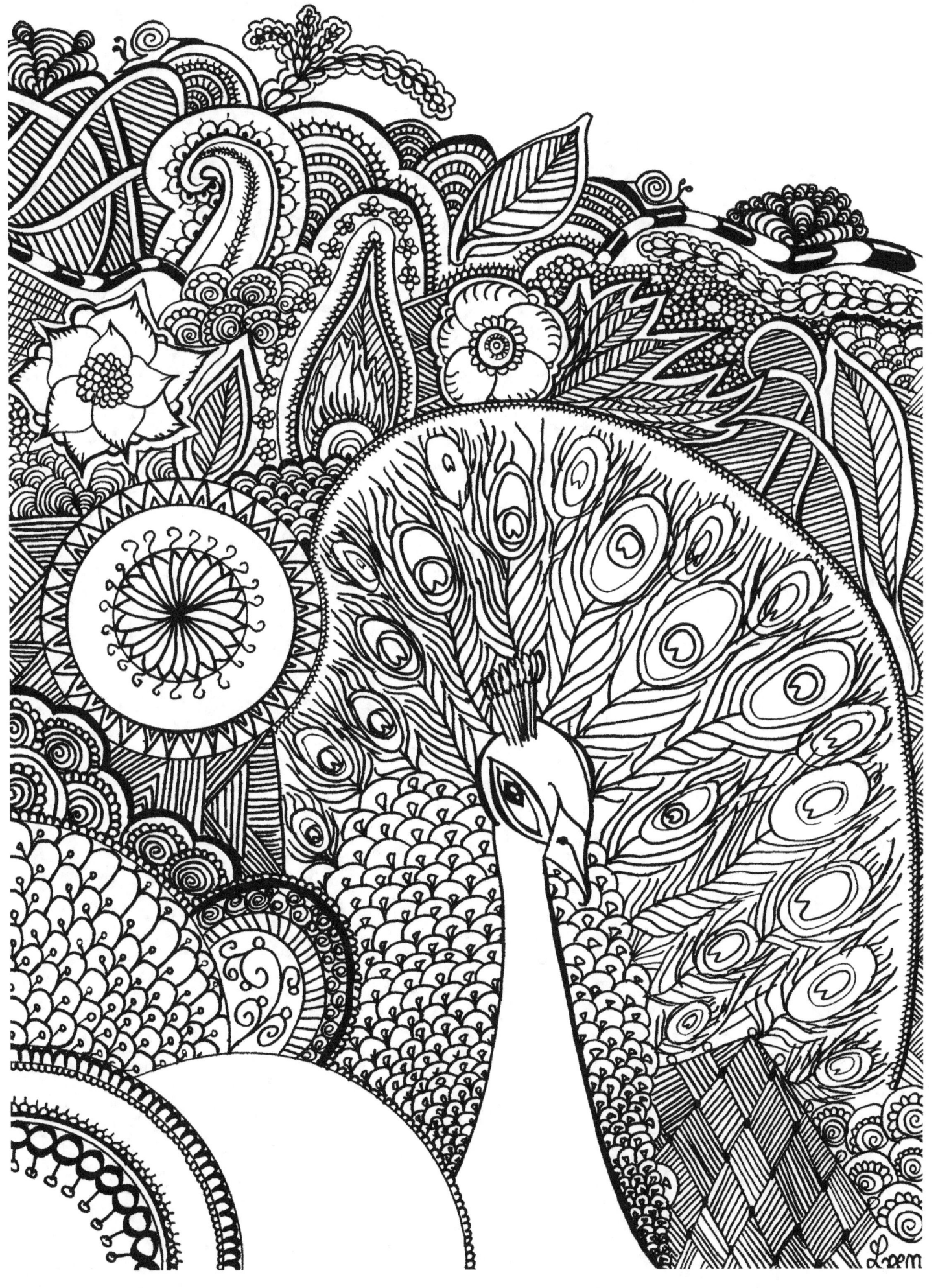

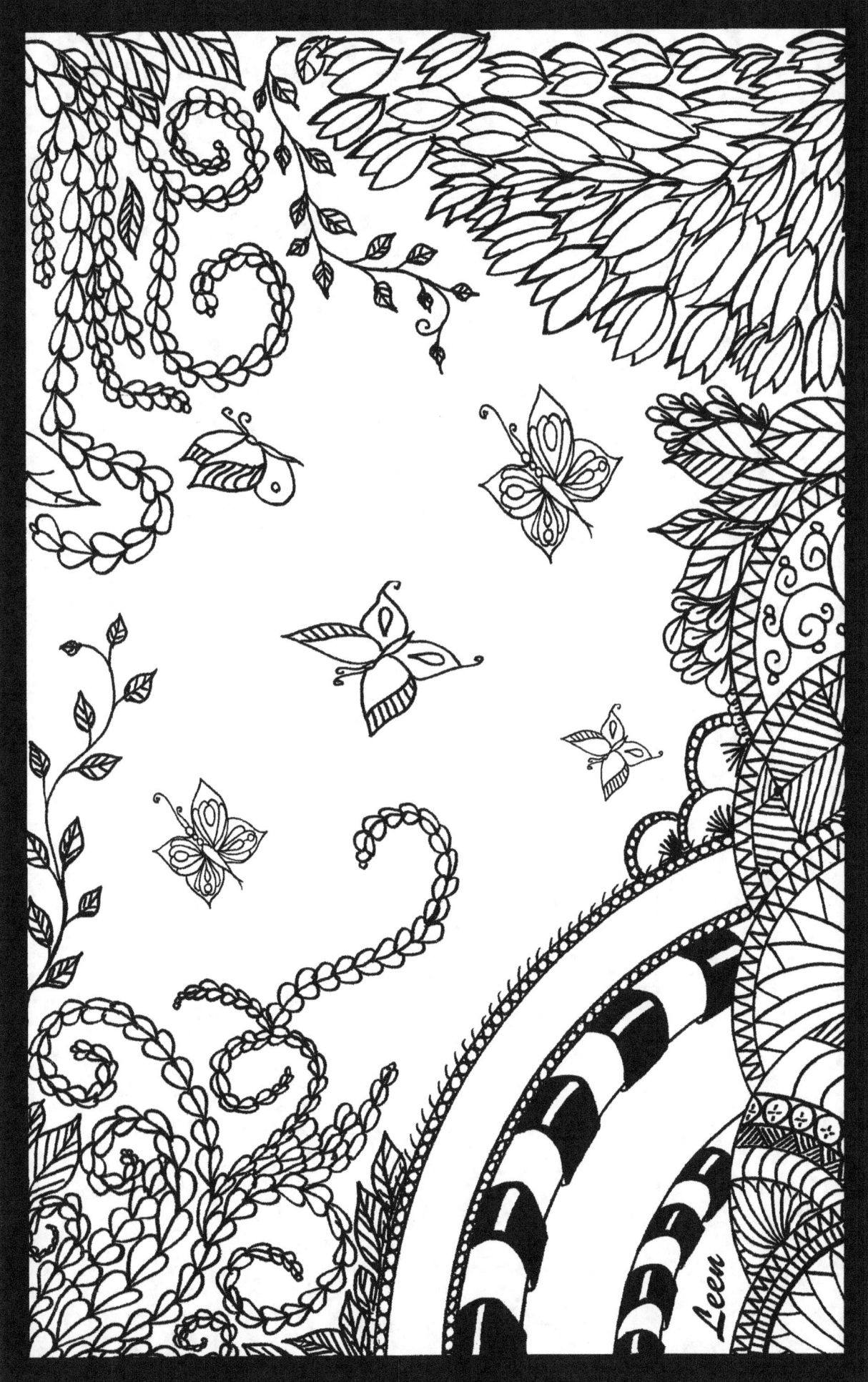

Fish kiss

Leen Margot

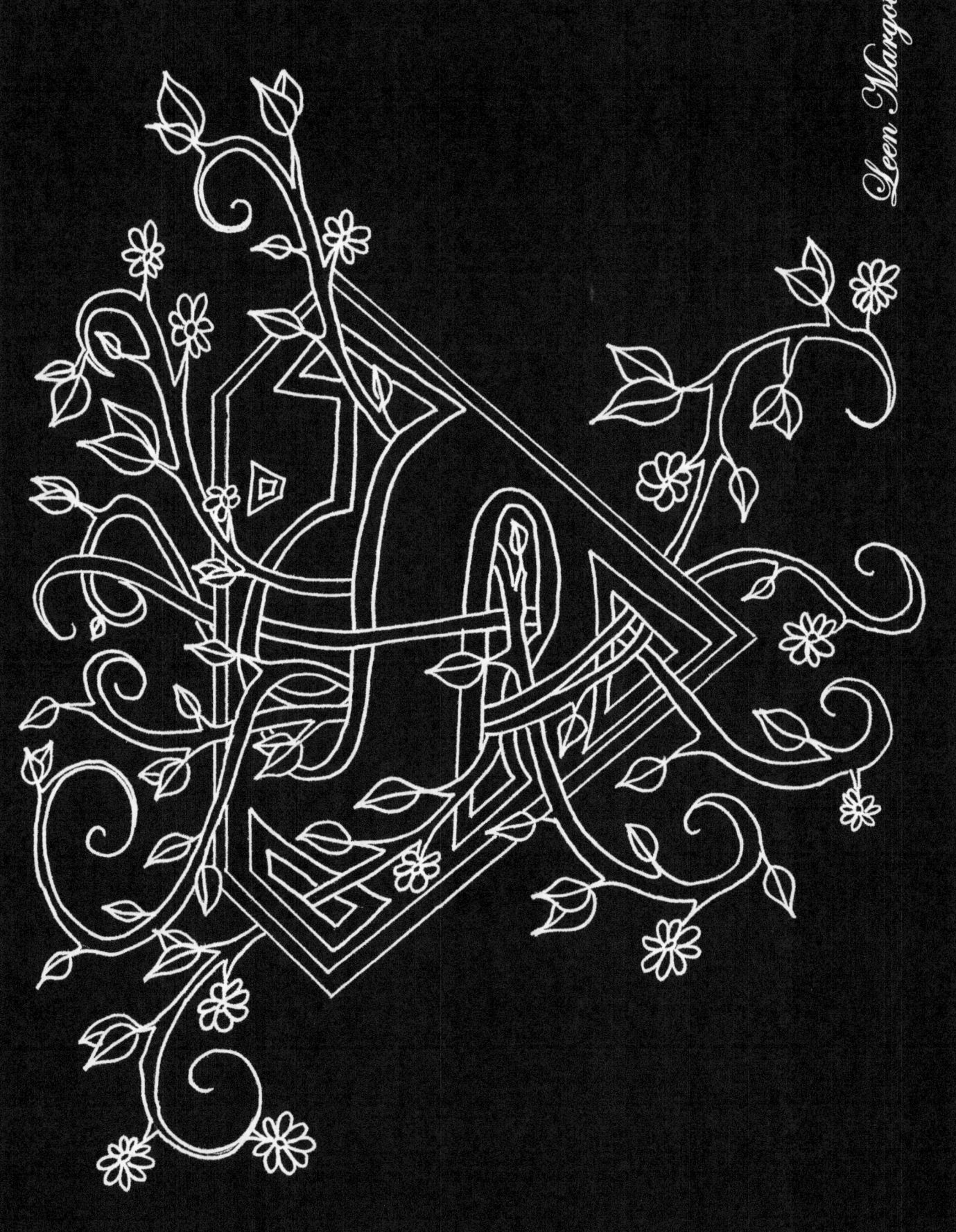

Coloring by Véro Pignot

Published by "GDG" Global Doodle Gems

Coloring by Leen Margot

www.ingramcontent.com/pod-product-compliance
Lightning Source LLC
Chambersburg PA
CBHW082215220526
45470CB00010B/3173

Drawn & colored by Nancy Sutton Lewin

Drawn & colored by Shelly Eartha Simpson

Global Doodle Gems Volume 6
"The Ultimate international Coloring Book...an Epic Collection from Artists around the World!"

Drawn by Arthur Santiago & Colored by Laurence Roucou

Drawn & colored by Mr End

Drawn & colored by Diane Pick-Ross

Drawn & colored by Judy West

Drawn & colored by Laurie Beauchamp

Drawn & colored by Dawn Miller

Drawn & colored by Alexandra Rodriguez

Drawn by Joseph Shivery & Colored by Taaroa Jay

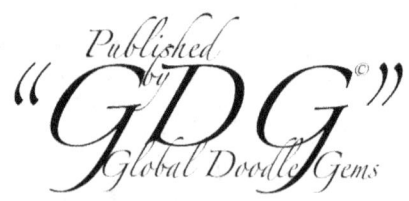

Share your colored versions with us ! We love seeing your results and hearing from you we are social !

The Official FB book page, stay on top of what we have in the works !
www.facebook.com/globaldoodlegems

The Community group, share your colored pages, meet the artists, enjoy exclusive freebies, take part in community Charity books and so much more......
www.facebook.com/groups/globaldoodlegems/

Follow us on Twitter.... @GlobalDoodlegem

We are on Instagram too
@globaldoodlegems for instagram

...and if you are not social like that we have a blog
globaldoodlegems.wordpress.com

Copyright © 2015 Global Doodle Gems

All rights are reserved by Global Doodle Gems.

Duplication of pages for personal use are allowed. You are invited to color the pages then scan/post your coloured versions to social networks, mentioning the book title and author/artist (Global Doodle Gems).

All artwork and images are protected by copyright laws. This book or any portion thereof may not, otherwise, be reproduced and/or distributed or transmitted without the express written permission of the artist/publisher of Global Doodle Gems.

All of us from the Global Doodle Gems wish you a colortastic time and look forward to seeing your wonderful color results online !